Choral Music in Nineteenth-Century America

A Guide to the Sources

N. Lee Orr
W. Dan Hardin

The Scarecrow Press, Inc.
Lanham, Maryland, and London
1999

SCARECROW PRESS, INC.

Published in the United States of America
by Scarecrow Press, Inc.
4720 Boston Way, Lanham, Maryland 20706
http://www.scarecrowpress.com

4 Pleydell Gardens, Folkestone
Kent CT20 2DN, England

Copyright © 1999 by N. Lee Orr and W. Dan Hardin

British Library Cataloguing in Publication Information Available

Library of Congress Cataloging-in-Publication Data

Orr, N. Lee, 1949–
    Choral music in nineteenth-century America : a guide to the
sources / N. Lee Orr, W. Dan Hardin.
        p.   cm.
    Includes bibliographical references and index.
    ISBN 0-8108-3664-5 (cloth : alk. paper)
    1. Choral music—United States—19th century Bibliography.
I. Hardin, W. Dan, 1950–   . II. Title.
ML128.C48O77 1999
016.7825'0973'09034-dc21   99-31630
                                                         CIP

⊖™ The paper used in this publication meets the minimum requirements of
American National Standard for Information Sciences—Permanence of
Paper for Printed Library Materials, ANSI/NISO Z39.48–1992.
Manufactured in the United States of America.

Contents

Contents

Preface

Choral music played a central role in American cultural life during the nineteenth century. It appealed to the country's sense of democratic values in that the choral experience was open to all, whether as singer or listener. It also functioned as a major signifyer of middle-class values. The standard bearer of choral music, the church choir, was one of the most revered institutions in American culture. The anthem--the sole province of the choir--provided rich musical solace to many each Sunday. Its comforting music and uplifting texts did much to soften the harsh realities of a society dominated by the competitive marketplace. With the rise of the urban middle class after mid-century came a rapid expansion in the number and grandeur of American churches. The affluent members marked their new status by supporting growing music programs, which showcased large choirs anchored by a professional quartet, as well as magnificent new pipe organs. All these new choristers each needed a copy of the anthem (or cantata) for each Sunday, which created a virtually unstoppable market for new works. By the end of the century many Americans found their most constant musical experiences in the services and music of their church.

Likewise, the community choral society enjoyed widespread support across class and ethnic lines. Its secular works—cantatas, part-songs, and oratorios—gave voice to the dominant cultural themes of Romanticism and Triumphalism. After mid-century amateur groups sprang up in virtually every city with more than thousand souls. Rare was the community that did not have some type of Beethoven or Mozart Club, oratorio society, male chorus, or choral union.

Throughout the country, from villages to major cities, these musical groups played a central role in the construction of American Victorian musical culture. Recently arrived German immigrants formed singing societies as soon as they could get settled, and by the end of century nearly 1,000 could be found across the land. "American" singing societies evolved from the glee clubs based on English models. The leader here was the Mendelssohn Club, which started in 1866 in New York with eight members. Oratorio societies followed, mainly in the larger cities. Perhaps the best known of these was the New York Oratorio Society, established in 1873 by Leopold Damrosch. American choral festivals, organized on English and German models, accelerated the growing enthusiasm for choral music. The 1872 Boston Peace Jubilee led by Patrick S. Gilmore set the record for notorious extravagance with a chorus of 20,000 and an orchestra of 2,000. In the subsequent years through World War I, choral music became an integral part of the American experience.

Yet this fact remains largely forgotten today. As early as 1918 Oscar Sonneck realized how quickly we were losing our own heritage. His plea for further study remains just as unheeded today:

> Whoever has had to occupy himself with our recent histories of music in America, will have noticed the scant courtesy shown to the first half of the nineteenth century. By paraphrased repetition of what Ritter, Mathews and others knew and by utilization of a few recent monographs on special subjects, the fact is more or less cleverly concealed that we know comparatively little about the historical currents and under-currents of that period. Certain phenomena like Lowell Mason's activity or Garcia's importation of Italian opera, or the Handel and Haydn Society, stand out prominently, surrounded by the names of sundry pioneers in the realm of higher art; but a cross-section of our historical knowledge of that period would reveal a rather brittle surface.[1]

Sonneck's words still ring true: we know comparatively little about choral music in nineteenth-century America. Most of the same topics from his era remain the central focus of investigation: Lowell Mason,

---

1. Oscar G. Sonneck, "The History of Music in America. A Few Suggestions," in *Miscellaneous Studies in the History of Music* (1921; reprint, New York: AMS Press, 1970): 339.

Italian Opera, Victorian hymnody, and the Handel and Haydn Society. The present-day scholarly pilgrim still echoes Sonneck's observation: "More and more I received the impression that the first half of the nineteenth century and no longer the eighteenth century is the mysterious period in our musical past, apart from its total pregnant importance for the future . . ." (p. 341). Indeed, choral music for the entire nineteenth century still awaits serious investigation, something that the noted bibliographical scholar, D. W. Krummel, argues emphatically in his fine *Bibliographical Handbook of American Music*: "Herein lies the greatest challenge to America's music bibliographers today." Concerning music from 1826 to 1900, Krummel states that "by the end of the nineteenth century, clearly (1) a great deal of music of all kinds had been published, although (2) we really do not know how much there was, because (3) it is under practically no bibliographical control, in the absence of even a first generation of work on most of it."[2]

This guide will play a seminal role in defining the entire field as it is the first complete survey of choral music in nineteenth-century America. It offers the only map of this territory, and for the first time brings some bibliographical control to this remarkable body of music. Even so, we still do not know how much music was published, what found a place in the contemporary repertory, what enjoyed only passing popularity, how the music was disseminated and received, how it was performed, and many other questions. Much of the music remains uncataloged in various seminary and historical society libraries, forgotten church choir collections, and private family papers. The bibliographic record likewise lies scattered all over the scholarly landscape and must be unearthed from the numerous periodicals, journals, biographies, newspapers, tracts, church histories, city histories, diaries, and correspondence of the period. Most of the material presented here was gathered from more than ten years of travel and research.

This guide focuses on the literature pertinent to *choral* music in the United States from the end of the second decade of the nineteenth century through the early years of the twentieth century. By *choral* music we mean music conceived, written, published, rehearsed, and performed by an ensemble of singers gathered specifically to present the music before an audience or congregation. This definition excludes

---

2. Urbana and Chicago: University of Illinois Press, 1987: 15.

that other great body of nineteenth-century American sacred vocal music, the hymn (including here the spiritual and gospel song and shape-note tunes), which served as music of all the people, not just a trained few. Making a categorical separation between the genres is elusive because church musicians of the period rarely drew clear distinctions. They used what materials they had for the immediate service at hand, unconcerned as to its source or original intent. For example, numerous four-part sacred works continued to be published in varying tunebook formats well into the second half of the century, supposedly for congregational use. How many of these were intended as anthems for the choir, and how many were simply newly composed hymns for the congregation? The answer changes from place to place and with each publication. For our purposes, we selected materials whose title or discussion focused on choral music and its genres.

This said, we cite important sources for the study of hymnology in recognition of the centrality that the Protestant hymn held for American life during the last century. The hymn became one of the most enduring cultural icons of the period. For Victorian Americans of all faiths and backgrounds, it served as one of the primary facilitators of Anglo-Saxon assimilation through its English language texts, simple melodic style, and shared imagery. These chapters provide the most important sources for beginning further investigation. No attempt at any kind of bibliographical completeness was attempted, as this would result in a volume so unwieldy as to eclipse the goal here of producing a workable-sized bibliography. Moreover, the hymns so beloved by Victorian Americans have already received broad and detailed attention in many fine studies.

This guide also provides individual chapters on the leading nineteenth-century composers who proved significant for the development of American choral music, beginning with Lowell Mason. As with a bibliography on the hymn, the bibliography on Mason is so extensive that we include only the major scholarly sources on his work, most important the thorough study done by Carol Pemberton. For the other composers, the bibliographies found in the works listed offer detailed references and citations of further documentation. Since all of these composers (with the exception of Mason) worked mainly during the second half of the century, the chapters are listed in alphabetical order by last name. Conspicuously absent here is material on one of the major American composers who began his work during the last part of the century: Charles Ives. We do not include him here as Ives's work remained largely unknown until well into the twentieth century and exerted virtually no influence on Victorian American choral music. The record of American choral music during the nineteenth century remains dispersed in the journals, newspapers, and periodicals of the era. While these began first appearing sporadically during the 1830s, by the time of the Civil War the trickle began turning into a stream then approached a torrent by century's end. The sheer amount of this material still presents the major challenge to research on choral music of the period. The studies listed in chapter two display the thorough bibliographical profiles available for studying these publications. Gratefully, an increasing number of these periodicals is being made available through various media. Perhaps the most important here is the ongoing series *Nineteenth-Century American Music Periodicals on Microfilm*.

One difficult-to-find group of studies we include here is that of city, regional, and church histories. Religion played such an important role in American life during the nineteenth century, that many churches commissioned histories, which they subsequently published. Within these studies lies a rich source offering insight into how the American choir developed, its leadership, who comprised its membership, what it sang each Sunday, and how that music was received. Likewise in the secular sphere, the histories of cities and regions provide valuable insight into the role community choral groups, oratorio societies, and other vocal ensembles played in American life of the period. We conclude with a chapter on general essays, sermons, and talks on music written and published during the period.

With this study we offer for the first time initial bibliographic control over the vast field of nineteenth-century American choral music. We can now say that at least we know what we are talking about. This is only the beginning, however. Although it opens up the territory and charts its boundaries, much remains to be done. We hope our work encourages further exploration into this rich and neglected area of American life.

N. Lee Orr, W. Dan Hardin

Chapter 1

Reference Works

A. P. Heinrich Collection. Washington, DC: Library of Congress Music Division. N.d.

American Folklife Center. *Ethnic Recordings in America: A Neglected Heritage.* Washington, DC: Library of Congress, American Folklife Center, 1982.

The American Musical Directory, 1861. 1861. Reprint, with a new introduction by Barbara Owen. New York: Da Capo Press, 1980.

Anderson, Michael J. *A Classified Index of North American Doctoral Dissertations and Dissertation Projects on Choral Music, Completed or Currently in Progress, through 1989.* Lawton, OK: American Choral Directors Association, 1990.

A Bibliography on Music and the Church. National Council of the Churches of Christ in the U.S.A., prepared by Walter E. Buszin, Theodore M. Finney, and Donald M. McCorkle for the Commission on Music. New York: N.p., 1958.

Block, Adrienne Fried, and Carol Neuls-Bates, comps. and eds. *Women in American Music: A Bibliography of Music and Literature.* Westport, CT: Greenwood Press, 1979.

Brooklyn College. Institute for Studies in American Music. *American Music before 1865 in Print and on Records: A Biblio-Discography.* Brooklyn: Institute for Studies in American Music-Brooklyn College of the City University of New York, 1976.

1

_____. *Index of the Recorded Anthology of American Music (New World Records NW201-300).* Brooklyn: Institute for Studies in American Music—Brooklyn College of the City University of New York, 1980.

Brown, Rae Linda. *Music, Printed and Manuscripts, in the James Weldon Johnson Memorial Collection of Negro Arts and Letters: An Annotated Catalog.* New York: Garland, 1982.

Claghorn, Charles Eugene. *Biographical Dictionary of American Music.* West Nyack, NY: Parker Publishing Co., 1973.

Cohen, Norm, and Paul Wells. "Recorded Ethnic Music: A Guide to Resources, Printed and Recorded." *Ethnic Recordings: A Neglected Heritage.* Washington, DC: Library of Congress American Folklife Center, 1978.

DeVenney, David P. *American Masses and Requiems: A Descriptive Guide.* Berkeley, CA: Fallen Leaf Press, 1990.

_____. *Nineteenth Century American Choral Music: An Annotated Guide.* Berkeley, CA: Fallen Leaf Press, 1987.

Directory of American Women Composers. [Chicago]: National Federation of Music Clubs, 1970.

District of Columbia Historical Records Survey. *Bio-Bibliographical Index of Musicians in the United States of America since Colonial Times.* 2nd ed. Washington, DC: Music Section, Pan American Union, 1956.

Dox, Thurston J. *American Oratorios and Cantatas: A Catalog of Works Written in the United States from Colonial Times to 1985.* 2 vols. Metuchen, NJ: Scarecrow Press, 1986.

Eagon, Angelo. *Catalog of Published Concert Music by American Composers.* Supplement to the 2nd ed. Metuchen, NJ: Scarecrow Press, 1971-74.

Evans, Margaret R. *Sacred Cantatas: An Annotated Bibliography, 1960-1979.* Jefferson, NC: McFarland, 1982.

Finell, Judith Greenberg, comp. *American Music Center Library Catalog of Choral and Vocal Works.* New York: American Music Center Library, 1975.

Frances Hall Johnson Program Collection. Connecticut Historical Society, Hartford. Contains programs of musical events in Hartford from the middle of the nineteenth century to the early twentieth century.

Gammond, Peter, and Burnett James. *Music on Record: A Critical Guide*. Vol. 4—Opera and Vocal Music. Westport, CT: Greenwood Press, 1978.

George Hodges Collection Finding Aid. Washington, DC: Library of Congress Music Division. Music (manuscript and printed) and writings by Edward Hodges and his son, John Sebastian Bach Hodges (1830-1915), and Faustina Hasse Hodges (1823-1895). Mostly sacred music.

Hall, Charles J. *A Chronicle of American Music, 1700-1995*. New York: Schirmer Books, 1996.

Harry Rowe Shelley Papers. New York: Academy of Arts and Letters Library. Contains about 200 items from the late nineteenth and early twentieth century.

Hartley, Kenneth R. *Bibliography of Theses and Dissertations in Sacred Music*. Detroit: Information Coordinators, 1967. (Detroit Studies in Music Bibliography, vol. 9.)

Heintze, James R. *American Music Studies: A Classified Bibliography of Master's Theses*. Detroit: Information Coordinators 1984. (Detroit Studies in Music Bibliography, vol. 8.)

_____. *Early American Music: A Research and Information Guide*. New York: Garland Publishing, 1990.

Horn, David. *The Literature of American Music in Books and Folk Music Collections: A Fully Annotated Bibliography*. Metuchen, NJ: Scarecrow Press, 1977.

Horn, David, with Richard Jackson. *The Literature of American Music in Books and Folk Music Collections: A Fully Annotated Bibliography*. Supplement 1. Metuchen, NJ: Scarecrow Press, 1988.

Marco, Guy A. *The Literature of American Music III, 1983-1992*. Lanham, MD: Scarecrow Press, 1996.

Marco, Guy A. *Checklist of Writings on American Music, 1640-1992*. Lanham, MD: Scarecrow Press, 1996.

Hovland, Michael, comp. *Musical Settings of American Poetry: A Bibliography*. Westport, CT: Greenwood Press, 1986.

Hubbard, William Lines, ed. *American History and Encyclopedia of Music*. 12 vols. Toledo, OH: Squire Cooley Co., 1910.

Jackson, Richard. *United States Music: Sources of Bibliography and Collective Biography.* ISAM Monograph No. 1. New York: Department of Music, Brooklyn College, City University of New York, 1973.

Johnson, H. Earle. *First Performances in America to 1900: Works with Orchestra.* Detroit: Published for the College Music Society by Information Coordinators, 1979.

Krummel, D. W. *Bibliographical Handbook of American Music.* Urbana and Chicago: University of Illinois Press, 1987.

_____. *Bibliographical Inventory to the Early Music in the Newberry Library, Chicago.* Boston: G. K. Hall, 1977.

Krummel, D. W., Jean Geil, Doris J. Dyen, and Deane L. Root. *Resources of American Music History: A Directory of Source Materials from Colonial Times to World War II.* Urbana: University of Illinois, 1981.

Loftis, Deborah C. *The Hymn. Index. Volume 1 (1949)–Volume 32 (1981).* Springfield, OH: The Hymn Society of America, Inc., 1982.

Mead, Rita H. *Doctoral Dissertations in American Music: A Classified Bibliography.* Brooklyn, NY: Institute for Studies in American Music, 1974.

Music for the Nation. American Sheet Music. An online collection of more than 22,000 musical compositions registered for copyright with the Library of Congress during the years 1870 to 1879. It includes much sacred and secular choral music. At http://memory. loc.gov/ammem/smhtml/smhome.html.

National Federation of Music Clubs. *Directory of American Women Composers.* [Chicago]: National Federation of Music Clubs, 1970.

Newland-Zeuner Collection Finding Aid. Washington, DC: Library of Congress Music Division. Materials from 1775 to 1885. Constitutes the working library of William A. Newland, who was active in many different musical circles in nineteenth-century Philadelphia. Mostly music, manuscript and printed.

Powell, Martha C. *A Selected Bibliography of Church Music and Music Reference Materials.* Louisville, KY: Southern Baptist Theological Seminary, 1977.

Samuel Warren Collection Finding Aid. Washington, DC: Library of Congress Music Division. Correspondence, concert and recital programs, church bulletins, and related materials collected either by Warren or given to him by his students, colleagues, and others in New York City and throughout the United States. Spans the years 1850 to 1914.

Skowronski, JoAnn. *Women in American Music: A Bibliography.* Metuchen, NJ: Scarecrow Press, 1978.

Spottswood, Richard K. *Ethnic Music on Records: A Discography of Ethnic Recordings Produced in the United States, 1893-1942.* Urbana: University of Illinois Press, 1990.

von Ende, Richard Chaffey. *Church Music: An International Bibliography.* Metuchen, NJ: Scarecrow Press, 1980.

W. B. Bradbury Collection Finding Aid. Washington, DC: Library of Congress Music Division. Contains holograph and first-edition printed musical scores, an unpublished biography by his granddaughter, Elma Marvin, a biographical letter written in 1928 by his son, correspondence relative to Bradbury's music publications during the early 1860s, and photographs. All musical compositions are secular.

Wilson, Bernard E., comp. *The Newberry Library Catalog of Early American Printed Sheet Music.* Boston: G. K. Hall, 1983.

Chapter 2

Periodical Bibliographies and Indexes

Adkins, Nelson F., ed. *Early American Periodicals Index to 1850.* New York: Readex Microprint, 1964. Library of Congress 65-594.

Annotated Guide to Periodical Literature on Church Music. 2 vols. Philadelphia: Music Article Guide, n.d. Covers years 1971 to 1972.

Berresford, Ronald Dale. "*The American Organist*: An Annotated Index to Volumes 1-17." Ph.D. diss., New York University, 1985.

[Charles Coffin Jewett.] "Appendix to the Librarian's Report: Copyright Publications Deposited prior to 1850 . . . Part II: List of Musical Compositions"; and " . . . for 1850 . . ."; in the *Fifth Annual Report of the Board of Regents* (Washington: Smithsonian Institution, 1851): 223-33 and 286-322.

Complete Catalogue of Sheet Music and Musical Works . . . 1870. New York: U.S. Board of Music Trade, 1871. Reprint, with a new introduction by Dena J. Epstein. New York: Da Capo, 1973.

Davison, Mary Veronica. "American Music Periodicals, 1853-1899." Ph.D. diss., University of Minnesota, 1973.

Flandorf, Vera S. "Music Periodicals in the United States: A Survey of Their History and Content." Master's thesis, University of Chicago, 1952.

Grimes, Calvin Bernard. "American Musical Periodicals, 1819-1852: Music Theory and Musical Thought in the United States." Ph.D. diss., University of Iowa, 1974.

Hammett, Thomas Foster. *The Choral Journal: An Annotated Index to Volumes 19-24 and a Comparison of Subject Material Published in Volumes 1-18 and Volumes 19-24.* Ed.D. diss., Florida State University, 1985.

Johnson, H. Earle. "Early New England Periodicals Devoted to Music." *Musical Quarterly* 26 (April 1940): 153-61.

Kinscella, Hazel G. "Americana Index to *the Musical Quarterly, 1915-1957.*" *Journal of Research in Music Education* 6, no. 2 (Fall 1958): 3-144.

Liebergan, Patrick Michael. "*Church Music:* An Annotated Bibliography and Index of Articles on Choral Music from 1966 to 1978." DMA diss., University of Colorado, 1980. (Also available from the American Choral Directors Association, Lawton, OK.)

Lowens, Irving. "Writings about Music in the Periodicals of American Transcendentalism." *Journal of the American Musicological Society* 10 (1957): 71-85.

Meggett, Joan M. *Music Periodical Literature: An Annotated Bibliography of Indexes and Bibliographies.* Metuchen, NJ: Scarecrow Press, 1978.

Millen, Irene. "American Musical Magazines, 1786-1865." Master's thesis, Carnegie Institute of Technology, 1949.

New Grove Dictionary of American Music. s.v. "Periodicals."

Paine, John Gordon. "*The Choral Journal:* An Index to Volumes 1-18." Lawton, OK: American Choral Directors Association, 1978.

Mussulman, Joseph A. *Music in the Cultured Generation: A Social History of Music in America, 1870-1900.* Evanston, IL: Northwestern University Press, 1971. Appendices 1-4 (pp. 200-73) list the contents of four major American periodicals.

Rash, Daniel. "1981-1985 Supplement to *A Classified, Annotated Bibliography of Articles Related to Choral Music in Five Major Periodicals through 1980.*" DMA diss., University of Colorado, 1988.

Repertoire International de la Presse Musicale: A Retrospective Index Series (RIPM). H. Robert Cohen, general ed. Ann Arbor, MI: University of Michigan Center for Studies in Nineteenth-Century Music, University of Maryland, 1988-.

Russell, Robert Jackson. *"The American Choral Review*: An Annotated Index of Volumes I-XX (1955-1979)." DMA diss., University of Colorado, 1979. (Also available from the American Choral Directors Association, Lawton, OK.)

Snodgrass, Isabel S. "American Musical Periodicals of New England and New York, 1786-1850." Master's thesis, Columbia University, Library School, 1947.

Stephens, Carol. "Descriptive Bibliography of American Music Magazines, 1866-1886." MLS thesis, Carnegie Institute of Technology, 1954.

Warner, Thomas E. *Periodical Literature on American Music, 1620-1920: A Classified Bibliography with Annotations.* Warren, MI: Harmonie Park Press, 1988.

Weichlein, William J. *A Checklist of American Music Periodicals, 1850-1900.* Detroit: Information Coordinators, 1970.

Whitten, Lynn, ed. *A Classified, Annotated Bibliography of Articles Related to Choral Music in Five Major Periodicals through 1980.* Lawton, OK: American Choral Directors Association, 1982.

Wunderlich, Charles. "A History and Bibliography of Early American Music Periodicals, 1782-1852." Ph.D. diss., University of Michigan, 1962.

Chapter 3

Miscellaneous Studies

Adler, Samuel. "Sacred Music in a Secular Age." In *Sacred Sound and Social Change: Liturgical Music in Jewish and Christian Experience*. Notre Dame, IN: Notre Dame University, 1992.

American Academy of Teachers of Singing. *Terminology in the Field of Singing*. New York: G. Schirmer, 1969.

"American Choral Composers Association." *The American Musician* 19, no. 1 (1890): 9.

American Musical Convention . . . with the Addresses, 1838. Boston: Kidder & Wright, [1838].

American Musical Convention. *Proceedings of the American Musical Convention Held in the Broadway Tabernacle on the 8th, 9th, and 10th of October, 1845: With the Addresses*. New York: Saxton & Miles, 1845.

"American Oratorios." *The Nation* 16, no. 398 (1873): 116-20.

Ammer, Christine. *Unsung: A History of Women in American Music*. Wesport, CT: Greenwood Press, 1980.

Bain, Wilfred Conwell. "The Status and Function of *A Cappella* Choirs in Colleges and Universities in the United States." Ed.D. diss., New York University, 1938.

Barnes, Edward S. "American Composers of Church Choral Music since 1876." *Music Teachers National Association Volume of Proceedings* 23. Hartford, CT: the Association, 1929: 101-19.

Beckel, James Cox. *The Church Manual: An Easy and Progressive Method for Acquiring a Knowledge of Church Music, Or the Organ, Cabinet Organ or Melodeon, Containing Psalms, Hymns, Chants, Anthems and Sentences, Arranged for Congregational Use, According to the Service of the P.E. Church.* Philadelphia: Lee & Walker, 1869.

Berg, David Eric. *Choral Music and the Oratorio.* New York: Caxton Institute, 1927.

Binder, Abraham Wolf. *The Jewish Music Movement in America: An Informal Lecture.* New ed. with additional resource information. New York: Jewish Music Council of the National Jewish Welfare Board, 1975.

Bissell, Joan B., and Susan S. Stanley. "History of the Cincinnati May Music Festivals, 1873-1971." *Official Program of the May Festival of Cincinnati 98th Anniversary Year, May 14, 15, 16, 21, 22, 1971.* Cincinnati: Cincinnati Musical Festival Association, 1971.

Bissell, Simeon. "The Oratorio of the Future." *American Art Journal* 60 (1892): 173-77.

Bolton, Jacklin Talmage. "Religious Influences on American Secular Cantatas, 1850-1930." Ph.D. diss., University of Michigan, 1964.

"Boy Choirs." *American Musician* 4, no. 4 (1887): 73.

Boyd, Charles N. "Choir Development since 1876, and the Preeminent Choirmasters." *Music Teachers National Association Proceedings* (1928): 67-80.

W. B. Bradbury. *Collection.* Library of Congress, Music Division. *See also chapter 1.*

"Brooklyn Choral Society." *American Musician.* 12, no. 10 (1889): 16.

Brooks, Henry M. *Olden-Time Music: A Compilation from Newspapers and Books.* 1888. Reprint, New York: AMS Press, 1973.

Cain, Noble. *Choral Music and Its Practice with Particular Reference to A Cappella Music.* New York: M. Witmark & Sons, 1932.

Campbell, Richard R. "Oratorio in America." Master's thesis, Kent State University, 1962.

"The Cantata." *Musical Herald* 8, no. 11 (1887): 331.

Carlson, Jon O. "The Performance of Choral Music in America from 1852 to 1872." *The Choral Journal* 14, no. 8 (April 1974): 20-21; no. 9 (May 1974): 5-8.

Carr, Samuel. *The Diary of Samuel Carr, Music Director at Old South Church, Boston, MA 1884-1904.* Held by Boston Public Library.

Chase, Gilbert. *America's Music, From the Pilgrims to the Present.* Rev. 3rd ed., with a foreword by Richard Crawford and a discographical essay by William Brooks. Urbana, IL: University of Illinois Press, 1992.

_____, ed. *The American Composer Speaks: A Historical Anthology, 1770-1965.* Baton Rouge: Louisiana State University Press, 1966.

Chester, Stephen M. "The Oratorio." *The Choral Advocate and Singing Class Journal* 2, no. 1 (1851): 5.

"Chorale Societies." *Musical Gazette* 4 (1854): 26.

Clark, J. Bunker. "The Beginnings of Bach in America." In *American Musical Life in Context and Practice to 1865.* New York: Garland, 1994.

Collins, Walter S. "What Is a Good Edition?" *The Choral Journal* 12, no. 3 (November 1971): 15-18.

Cozens, J. "An American Choral Music Heritage." *Choral Guide* 12 (March 1959): 16-19.

Damian, Ronald. "A Historical Study of the Caecilian Movement in the United States." DMA diss., Catholic University of America, 1984.

Damrosch, Frank. *Programs of the First Eight Seasons of the Musical Arts Society of New York.* New York: The Republican Press, for the Society, 1894-1901.

Davison, Archibald T. *Protestant Church Music In America.* Boston: E. C. Schirmer, 1933.

Decker, Harold A., and Julius Herford, eds. *Choral Conducting: A Symposium.* Englewood Cliffs, NJ: Prentice-Hall, 1973.

Delorenzo, Joseph P. "The Chorus in American Musical Theatre: Emphasis on Choral Performance." Ph.D. diss., New York University, 1985.

DeVenney, David P. *Source Readings in American Choral Music.* Missoula, MT: College Music Society, 1995.

Dickinson, Edward. *The History of Church Music: Syllabus, with Bibliographical References. . . .* Oberlin, OH: Pearce and Randolph, Printers, 1896.

_____. *Music in the History of the Western Church.* New York: Charles Scribner's Sons, 1902, 1931.

Douglas, Charles Winfred. *Church Music in History and Practice: Studies in the Praise of God.* 1937. Rev. by Leonard Ellinwood. London: Faber and Faber, 1962.

Drinker, S. H. "Music for Women's Choruses: The Nineteenth Century." *Music Clubs Magazine* 30 (April 1951): 6-7.

Dwight, John S. "On the Forty-Sixth Psalm." *Dwight's Journal of Music* 16 (May 1874): 231.

Edwards, Arthur C., and W. Thomas Marroco. *Music in the United States.* Dubuque: Brown, 1968.

Ehmann, Wilhelm. "Choral Music in the United States." *The Choral Journal* 12, no.1 (September 1971): 5-8.

Ellinwood, Leonard. "English Influences in American Church Music." *Proceedings of the Royal Musical Association* 80 (1953-54): 1-13.

_____. *The History of American Church Music.* New York: Morehouse-Gorham, 1953.

Elson, Louis Charles. *The History of American Music.* Rev. to 1925 by Arthur Elson. 1925. Reprint, New York: B. Franklin, 1971.

_____. *The History of American Church Music.* New York: B. Franklin, [1971].

Epstein, Dena J. *Music Publishing in Chicago before 1871: The Firm of Root & Cady, 1858-1871.* Detroit: Information Coordinators, 1969. (Detroit Studies in Music Bibliography, No. 14.)

Etherington, Charles L. *Protestant Worship Music; Its History and Practice.* New York: Holt, Rinehart and Winston, 1962.

Farwell, Arthur, and W. Dermot Darby, eds. *Music in America.* New York: National Society of Music, 1915. (*The Art of Music,* Daniel Gregory Mason, ed. Vol. 4.)

Faugerstrom, Eugene. "The Dramatic Function of the Chorus in English Oratorio from 1880 to the Present." Ph.D. diss., Northwestern University, 1964.

Fawcett-Yeske, Maxine Ann. "The Fuging Tune in America, 1770-1820: An Analytical Study." Ph.D. diss., University of Colorado at Boulder, 1997.

Finck, Henry T. *My Adventures in the Golden Age of Music.* New York: Funk & Wagnalls, 1926.

Fischer, William Arms. *Music Festivals in the United States: An Historical Sketch.* [Boston]: The American Choral and Festival Alliance, Inc., 1934.

Foster, Myles Birket. *Anthems and Anthem Composers: An Essay upon the Development of the Anthem from the Time of the Reformation to the End of the Nineteenth Century.* 1901. Reprint, New York: Da Capo Press, 1970.

Gabriel, Charles H. *Church Music of Yesterday, Today and for Tomorrow.* Chicago: Rodeheaver, 1921.

Garabrant, Maurice. "The Choirmaster and the Boy Choir in the Protestant Liturgical Church." Master's thesis, Union Theological Seminary, 1949.

Glass, James William. "The Sacred Art Song in the United States, 1869-1975." DMA diss., Southwestern Baptist Theological Seminary, 1976.

Gould, Nathaniel D. *Church Music in America, Comprising Its History and Its Peculiarities at Different Periods; With Cursory Remarks on Its Legitimate Use and Its Abuse; With Notices of the Schools, Composers, Teachers, and Societies.* 1853. Reprint, New York: AMS Press, 1971.

Gonzo, Carroll L. "Research in Choral Music: A Perspective." *Council for Research in Music Education Bulletin* 33 (Summer 1973): 21-31.

Hall, Roger. "Early Performances of Bach and Handel in America." *Journal of Church Music* 27, no. 5 (May 1985): 4-7.

Hastings, Thomas. *Dissertation of Musical Taste; or General Principles of Taste Applied to the Art of Music.* New introduction by James E. Dooley. 1822. Reprint, New York: Da Capo Press, 1974.

_____. *The History of Forty Choirs.* 1854. Reprint, New York: AMS Press, 1976.

Haweis, H. R. *Music and Morals.* 1872. Reprint, Freeport, NY: Books for Libraries Press, [1973]. This book exists in many reprints.

_____. "Oratorio and Drama." *Harper's Monthly* 30 (December 1889): 109-15.

Hewins, James M. *Hints Concerning Church Music, the Liturgy and Kindred Subjects.* Boston: Ide & Dutton, 1856.

Hilbrich, Paul D. "On the Alienation of Audiences." *The Choral Journal* 13, no. 5 (January 1973): 5-6.

Hitchcock, H. Wiley. "Sources for the Study of American Music," *American Studies International* 14, no. 2 (1975): 3-9.

Hodge, Charles Russell. *Clergy and Choir*. Milwaukee: Young Churchman Co., 1891.

Hodges, Edward. *An Essay on the Cultivation of Church Music*. New York: J. A. Sparks, 1841.

Hood, George. *A History of Music in New England: With Biographical Sketches of Reformers and Psalmists*. Boston: Wilkins, Carter, 1846.

Howard, John Tasker. *Our American Music: A Comprehensive History from 1620 to the Present*. 4th ed. New York: Thomas Y. Crowell, 1965.

Howe, Granville L., and William Smythe Babcock Mathews. *A Hundred Years of Music in America*. 1889. Reprint, New York: AMS Press, 1970.

Hubbard, W. L., ed. *History of American Music*. Toledo: Irving Squire, 1908. (*American History and Encylcopedia of Music*, vol. 4.)

Hughes, Rupert. *Contemporary American Composers, Being a Study of the Music of This Country, Its Present Conditions and Its Future, with Critical Estimates and Biographies of the Principal Living Composers. . . .* Boston: L. C. L. C. Page and Co., 1900.

_____. *American Composers: A Study of the Music of This Country, and of Its Future, with Biographies of the Leading Composers of the Present Time. Being a New Revised Edition of Contemporary American Composers*. With additional chapters by Arthur Elson. 1914. Reprint, New York: AMS Press, 1973.

Humphreys, Frank Landon. *The Evolution of Church Music*. New York: Little & Co., 1896.

Hungerford, Edward. *The American Book of Church Services with Selections for Responsive Readings and the Full Orders of Service for the Celebration of Matrimony, for Funerals, and Other Occasional Ministrations; Also an Ample List of Selections of Sacred Music, with References for the Guidance of Pastors and Choristers*. 2nd ed. Boston: Houghton-Mifflin, 1891.

Hungerford, E. "Church Music." *New Englander* 17 (July 1890): 56-63.

Hutchings, Arthur. *Church Music in the Nineteenth Century*. Westport, CT: Greenwood Press, 1977. Originally appeared in *Studies in Church Music*. London: H. Jenkins, 1967.

"Is Glee-Singing Sinful?" *American Musical Review and Choral Advocate* 3, no. 7 (1852): 104.

Jacobs, Arthur, ed. *Choral Music: A Symposium.* Baltimore: Penguin Books, 1966.

Johnson, H. Earle. "Longfellow and Music." *American Music Research Center Journal* 7 (1997). Entire issue.

_____. "The Need for Research in the History of American Music." *Journal of Research in Music Education* 6, no. 1 (Spring 1958): 43-61.

Jones, F. O., ed. *A Handbook of American Music and Musicians, Containing Biographies of American Musicians, and History of the Principal Musical Institutions, Firms and Societies.* 1886. Reprint, New York: Da Capo Press, 1971.

Jones, Maurice Allen. "American Theater Cantatas: 1852-1907." Ph.D. diss., University of Illinois at Urbana-Champaign, 1975.

Kaatrud, Paul G. "Revivalism and the Popular Spiritual Song in Mid-Nineteenth Century America: 1830-1879." Ph.D. diss., University of Minnesota, 1977.

Kegerreis, Richard Irl. "History of the High-School *A Cappella* Choir." Part VIII. *The Choral Journal* (January 1971): 12. History of the high school choir, ca. 1837-1920.

_____. "History of the High-School *A Cappella* Choir." Ph.D. diss., University of Michigan, 1964.

Kennel, Pauline Graybill. "Peter Christian Lutkin: Northwestern University's First Dean of Music." Ph.D. diss., Northwestern University, 1981.

Kent, Ralph McVety. "A Study of Oratorios and Sacred Cantatas Composed in America before 1900." Ph.D. diss., University of Iowa, 1954.

Kiver, Christopher. "Abundant Opportunity." *Choir & Organ* 3, no. 6 (December 1995): 15-17.

Kroeger, Karl. "The Church-Gallery Orchestra in New England." *American Music Research Center Journal* 4 (1994): 23-30.

Lahee, Henry C. *Annals of Music in America: A Chronological Record of Significant Musical Events from 1640 to the Present Day with Comments on the Various Periods into Which the Work Is Divided.* 1922. Reprint, New York: AMS Press, 1969.

Lang, Paul Henry. *One Hundred Years of Music in America.* New York: G. Schirmer, 1961.

Leavitt, D. L. "Secular Choral Music: A Survey." *Notes* 18, no. 4 (1961): 658-62.

Liemohn, Edwin. *The Singing Church*. Columbus, OH: Wartburg Press, 1959.

Lindsley, Charles Edward. "Early Nineteenth-Century American Collections of Sacred Choral Music, 1800-1819." Ph.D. diss., University of Iowa, 1968.

Lloyd, Frederick E. J., comp. *Lloyd's Church Musicians Directory: The Blue Book of Church Musicians in America*. 1910. Reprint, New York: AMS Press, 1974.

Lorenz, Ellen Jane. *'76 to '76: A Study of Two Centuries of Sacred Music in America, Based on and Illustrated from the E. S. Lorenz Collection of 350 Nineteenth-Century American Tune Books, Hymnals, Anthem Books, and Sunday School Songbooks*. Dayton, OH: Lorenz Publishing Co., 1975.

Lowens, Irving. *The Choral Music of America before the Civil War*. New York: New York Public Library, 1958.

_____. *Music in America and American Music: Two Views of the Scene, with a Bibliography of the Published Writings of Irving Lowens*. Brooklyn: Institute for Studies in American Music, Brooklyn College, 1978.

Lutkin, Peter C. "The Larger Choral Groups and Preeminent Choral Leaders since 1876." *Music Teachers National Association, Proceedings* 23 (1928): 81-100.

_____. *Music in the Church*. 1910. Reprint, New York: AMS Press, [1970].

McGlinchee, Claire. "American Literature in American Music." *Musical Quarterly* 31, no. 1 (January 1945): 101-19.

McPhee, Edward Wallace. "The Quartet Choir in the Worship Service." Master's thesis, Union Theological Seminary, 1931.

Martin, Edward L. "A Comparative Study of Non-Traditional Vocal Compositional Techniques Which Have Been Incorporated into Selected Dramatic Choral Works by Composers of the United States of America." DMA diss., University of Missouri-Kansas City, 1987.

Mathews, W. S. B. "Music in the 19th Century." *Music* 17 (1900): 233-45, 345-46, 459-82.

_____. "The Nineteenth Century and National Schools of Music." *Music* 19 (1901): 334-51.

Mattfeld, Julius. *Variety Music Cavalcade, 1620-1969: A Chronology of Vocal and Instrumental Music Popular in the United States.* 3rd ed. Englewood Cliffs: Prentice-Hall, 1971.

Mees, Arthur. *Choirs and Choral Music.* 1901. Reprint, New York: Greenwood Press, [1969].

Mellers, Wilfrid. *Music in a New Found Land: Themes and Developments in the History of American Music.* London: Barrie & Rockliff, 1964; New York: Knopf, 1965.

Metcalf, Frank J. *American Writers and Compilers of Sacred Music.* 1925. Reprint, New York: Russell & Russell, 1967.

Meyer, Ramon Eugene. "Oratorios by American Born Composers in the Eighteenth and Nineteenth Centuries." Master's thesis, University of Cincinnati, 1956.

Mize, Lou Stem. "A Study of Selected Choral Settings of Walt Whitman Poems." Ph.D. diss., Florida State University, 1967.

Muhlenberg, William Augustus. *A Primer on Church Musick.* New York: S. W. Benedict, [1845].

Mussulman, Joseph A. *Music in the Cultured Generation: A Social History of Music in America, 1870-1900.* Evanston, IL: Northwestern University Press, 1971.

"New Cantata." *American Music Journal* 2, no. 4 (1886): 4.

"New York Chorus Society." *American Musician* 18,no. 10 (1890): 12.

"New York Musical Matters: The Oratorio of Elijah." *Journal of the Fine Arts* 47 (1851): 151.

Newland, William Augustine. *Newland/Zeuner Collection.* Library of Congress, Music Division. *See also chapter 1.*

Osborne, William. "Five New England Gentlemen." *Music* 3, no. 8 (August 1969): 27-29.

Parmenter, R. "Americans Rediscover Their Voices." *New York Times,* section 2, 25 August 1957.

Phillips, Kenneth H. "Choral Music Comes of Age." *Music Educators Journal* 75, no. 4 (December 1988): 22.

Pohly, Linda Louise. "Welsh Choral Music in America in the Nineteenth Century." Ph.D. diss., Ohio State University, 1989.

Rasmussen, Jane. "A Philadelphia Dialogue on the Quality of Church Music, 1829." In *Sacra/Profana: Studies in Sacred and Secular Music for Johannes Riedel,* ed. Audrey Davidson and Clifford Davidson. Vol. 1. Minneapolis, MN: Friends of Minnesota Music, 1985.

_____. *Musical Taste as a Religious Question in Nineteenth Century America*. Lewiston, NY: E. Mellen Press, 1986.

Reid, Robert Addison. "Russian Sacred Choral Music and Its Assimilation into and Impact on the American *A Cappella* Choir Movement." DMA diss., University of Texas at Austin, 1983.

Rhoden, Dewey Clinton, Jr. "The Community-Oriented Boy-Choir in the United States." Ph.D. diss., Florida State University, 1972.

Ritter, Frederic Louis. *Music in America*. New York: Charles Scribners Sons, 1883.

Robinson, Ray, and Allen Winold. *The Choral Experience: Literature, Materials and Methods*. New York: Harper's College Press, 1976. Reprint, Prospect Heights, IL: Waveland Press, 1992.

Ryan, Thomas. *Recollections of an Old Musician*. 1899. Reprint, New York: Da Capo Press, 1979.

Sablosky, Irving. *What They Heard: Music in America, 1852-1881, from the Pages of Dwight's Journal of Music*. Baton Rouge: Louisiana State University Press, 1986.

Schauffler, Robert Haven, and Sigmund Spaeth. *Music as a Social Force in America and the Science of Its Practice*. New York: The Caxton Institute, Inc., 1927.

Skinner, Ellouise W. "Sacred Music at Union Theological Seminary, 1836-1953: An Informal History." Master's thesis, Union Theological Seminary, 1953.

Starling, Leonard Bryan, Jr. "A Survey and Analysis of the Protestant Chapel Music Program of the Armed Forces of the United States." DMA diss., Southern Baptist Theological Seminary, 1970.

Steese, Ruth Zimmerman. "Choral Music in American Colleges." Master's thesis, Eastman School of Music, University of Rochester, 1934.

Stevenson, Robert M. "American Musical Scholarship: Parker to Thayer." *19th Century Music* 1, no. 3 (March 1978): 191-210.

_____. "Church Music: A Century of Contrasts." In *One Hundred Years of Music in America*. New York: G. Schirmer, 1961.

_____. *Patterns of Protestant Church Music*. Durham, NC: Duke University Press, 1953.

_____. *Protestant Church Music in America: A Short Survey of Men and Movements from 1564 to the Present*. New York: Norton, 1970.

Stone, J. H. "Mid-Nineteenth-Century American Beliefs in the Social Values of Music." *Musical Quarterly* 43 (January 1957): 38-49.

Stopp, Jacklin Bolton. "The Secular Cantata in the United States: 1850-1919." *Journal of Research in Music Education* 17, no. 14 (Winter 1969): 388-98.

Topel, Michael. "Der Chor in Porgy and Bess." *Musik und Bildung* 19, no. 12 (1987): 938-41.

Upton, George Putnam. *The Standard Cantatas: Their Stories, Their Music, and Their Composers, A Handbook.* 6th ed. Chicago: A. C. McClurg, 1897.

_____. *The Standard Concert Guide: A Handbook of the Standard Symphonies, Oratorios, Cantatas, and Symphonic Poems for the Concert Goer.* Chicago: A. C. McClung and Co., 1908.

_____. *The Standard Oratorios: Their Stories, Their Music, and Their Composers: A Handbook.* Chicago: A. C. McClung and Co., 1887.

Van Camp, Leonard W. "The Development of the Present Status of *A Cappella* Singing in United States Colleges and Universities." DMA diss., University of Missouri at Kansas City, 1964.

_____. "Nineteenth Century Choral Music in America: A German Legacy." *American Choral Review* 23, no. 4 (October 1981): 5-12.

_____. "The Rise of American Choral Music and the *A Cappella* 'Bandwagon.'" *Music Educators Journal* 67, no. 3 (November 1980): 36-40.

Vincent, Marvin Richardson. *Church Music.* New York: A. S. Barnes, [18??].

Weaver, Paul John. *A Study Outline: Sacred Choral Music.* Ithaca, NY: Music Clubs Magazine, 1938.

Weller, Philip T. "Early Church Music in the United States." *Caecilia* 66 (1939): 297-304.

Wienandt, Elwyn A., *Choral Music of the Church.* New York: The Free Press, 1965. Reprint, New York: Da Capo Press, 1980.

_____. *Opinions on Church Music: Comments and Reports from Four and a Half Centuries.* Waco, TX: Markham Press Fund of Baylor University Press, 1974.

Wienandt, Elwyn A., and Robert Young. *The Anthem in England and America.* New York: The Free Press, 1970.

Willis, Richard Storrs. *Church Chorals and Choir Studies.* New York: Clark, Austin, & Smith, 1850.

_____. "Descriptive Choir Singing." *The Musical World and Times* 8, no. 2 (1854): 13.

_____. *Our Church Music: A Book for Pastors and People.* New York: Dana and Co., 1856.

Wilson, Ruth Mack. *Anglican Chanting in England, Scotland, and America, 1660-1820.* Oxford: Clarendon Press; New York: Oxford University Press, 1996.

Wolfe, Richard J. *Secular Music in America, 1801-1825: A Bibliography.* 3 vols. New York: New York Public Library, Astor, Lenox and Tilden Foundations, 1964.

Young, Percy. *The Choral Tradition.* New York: W. W. Norton, 1981.

Chapter 4

Moravian Music

Ballenger, Larry Desmond. "The Music of the Moravians." Master's thesis, Fresno State College, 1967.

Boeringer, James. "Frances Florentine Hagen." *Journal of Church Music* 24, no. 8 (October 1982): 2-3.

_____. "Handel and the Moravians." *Journal of Church Music* 27, no. 2 (February 1985): 6-9.

_____. "Haydn's Herrn Hutters." *Moravian Music Journal* 29, no. 1 (1984): 14-20.

_____. "Johann Christian Bechler." *Journal of Church Music* 25, no. 6 (June 1983): 7.

_____. "Moravian Composers' Series: Johann Friedrich Peter." *Journal of Church Music* 26 (December 1984): 10-12.

_____. *Morning Star: The Life and Works of Francis Florentine Hagen (1815-1907), Moravian Evangelist and Composer.* Winston-Salem, NC: Moravian Music Foundation, 1986.

Claypool, Richard D. "Archival Collection of the Moravian Music Foundation and Some Notes on the Philharmonic Society of Bethlehem." *Fontes Artis Musicae* 23, no. 4 (October-December 1976): 177-90.

Cumnock, Frances, ed. *Catalog of the Salem Congregation Music.* Chapel Hill: University of North Carolina Press, 1980.

David, Hans T. *Musical Life in the Pennsylvania Settlements of the Unitas Fratrum.* With a foreword by Donald M. McCorkle. Winston-Salem: Moravian Music Foundation Press, 1959.

Falconer, Joan O. "The Second Berlin Song School in America." *Musical Quarterly* 59, no. 3 (July 1973): 411-40.

Flannagan, William Patrick. "A Performing Edition and Study of the Unpublished Concerted Anthems of John Antes (1740-1811)." Ph.D. diss., Catholic University of America, 1995.

Gombosi, Marilyn, ed. *Catalog of the Johannes Herbst Collection.* Chapel Hill: University of North Carolina Press, 1970.

_____. *A Day of Solemn Thanksgiving: Moravian Music for the Fourth of July, 1783, in Salem, N.C.* Chapel Hill: University of North Carolina Press, 1977.

Hall, Harry H. "Moravian Music Education in America, ca. 1750 to ca. 1830." *Journal of Research in Music Education* 29, no. 3 (Fall 1981): 225-34.

Hartzell, Lawrence. *Ohio Moravian Music.* Winston-Salem: Moravian Music Foundation Press, 1988.

Hellyer, Roger. "The Harmoniemusik of the Moravian Communities in America." *Fontes Artis Musicae* 27, no. 2 (April-June 1980): 95-108.

Herbst, Johannes. *The Johannes Herbst Collection: c. 1752-1812 / The Moravian Music Foundation Archives, Winston-Salem.* New York: University Music Editions, 1976. Microfiche.

Hertel, Marilyn. "The Development of the Moravian Sacred Music." Master's thesis, Bob Jones University, 1968.

Hoople, Donald Graham. "Moravian Music Education and the American Moravian Music Tradition." Ed.D. diss., Columbia University, 1976.

Howe, M. A. DeWolfe. "'Venite in Bethlehem': The Major Chord." *Musical Quarterly* 28, no. 2 (April 1942): 174-85.

Huebener, Mary A. "Bicentennial History of the Lititz Moravian Congregation." *Transactions of the Moravian Historical Society* 14 (1947-51): 199-271.

Ingram, Jeannine. "Music in American Moravian Communities: Transplanted Traditions in Indigenous Practices." *Communal Societies* 2 (Autumn 1982): 39-51.

Ingram, Peter J. "A Musical Potpourri: The Commonplace Book of Johann Friedrich Peter." *Moravian Music Journal* 24, no. 1 (1979): 2-7+.

John, Robert W., and Irving Lowens. *A Catalogue of the Irving Lowens Collection of Tune Books: Moravian Music Foundation, Winston Salem, North Carolina.* [Athens]: University of Georgia, 1971.

Johansen, J. H. "The Hymnody of the Moravian Church." *Hymn* 8, no. 2 (April 1957): 41-46, 59.

_____. "Moravian Hymnody." *Hymn* 30, no. 3 (1979): 167-77, 195, 30; no. 4 (1979): 230-39, 242.

Jones, Perry. "The Bethlehem Bach Choir Approaches Its Centennial." *The Choral Journal* 34, no. 9 (April 1994): 13-18.

Konig, Linda. "Our Musical Heritage from the Moravians." *Church Musician* 27, no. 9 (June 1976): 40-45.

Kortz, Edwin W. "The Liturgical Development of the American Moravian Church." *Transactions of the Moravian Historical Society* 18 (1961-62): 267-302.

Kroeger, Karl. "A Core Repertory of American Moravian Hymn-Tunes." *Moravian Music Journal* 31, no. 1 (Spring 1986): 2-8.

_____. "David Moritz Michael's Psalm 103: An Early American Sacred Cantata." *Moravian Music Foundation Bulletin* 21, no. 2 (Fall-Winter 1976): 10-11.

_____. "The Johannes Herbst Collection: The Complete Collection of Manuscripts as Found in the Archives of the Moravian Music Foundation, Winston-Salem, N.C." (Review.) *Notes* 37, no. 2 (December 1980): 398-99.

_____. "The Moravian Choral Tradition: Yesterday and Today." *The Choral Journal* 19, no. 5 (January 1979): 5-9, 12.

_____. "Moravian Music in America: A Survey." In *Unitas Fratrum: Herrnhuter Studien.* ed. Mari P. van Buijtenen and others. Utrecht: Rijksarchie, 1975.

Lawson, Charles Truman. "Musical Life in the Unitas Fratum Mission at Springplace, Georgia, 1800-1936." Ph.D. diss., Florida State University, 1970.

Maurer, Joseph A. "America's Heritage of Moravian Music: Contributions of Early Pennsylvania Composers." *Historical Review of Berks County* 18 (April-June 1953): 66-70, 87-91.

McCorkle, Donald. M. "The Moravian Contribution to American Music." *Notes* 13 (September 1956): 597-606.

_____. "Moravian Music in Salem: A German-American Heritage." Ph.D. diss., Indiana University, 1958.

Nolte, Ewald V. "Choral Music in the Moravian Archives." *American Choral Review* 9, no. 1 (1966): 6, 18.

Poole, Franklin Parker. "The Moravian Musical Heritage: Johann Christian Geisler's Music in America." Ph.D. diss., George Peabody College for Teachers, 1971.

Pruett, James Worrell. "Francis Florentine Hagen, American Moravian Musician." Master's thesis, University of North Carolina at Chapel Hill, 1957.

Ramsey, Darhyl S. "Sources for Research into Moravian Music. I: Dissertations." *Moravian Music Journal* 41, no. 2 (Fall 1996): 23-28.

_____. "Resources for Study of Moravian Music. II: The Music Index." *Moravian Music Journal* 42, 1 (Spring 1997): 12-22.

Rau, Albert G., and Hans David. *A Catalog of Music by American Moravians, 1742-1842, from the Archives of the Moravian Church at Bethlehem, Pennsylvania.* 1938. Reprint, New York: AMS Press, 1970.

Reed, Tracey L. "Johann Christian Bechler, Moravian Minister and Composer: The American Years, 1806-1836." Master's thesis, Indiana University of Pennsylvania, 1973.

Roberts, Dale Alexander. "The Sacred Vocal Music of David Moritz Michael: An American Moravian Composer." DMA diss., University of Kentucky, 1978.

Rothrock, Donna K. "Moravian Music Education: Forerunner to Public School Music." *Bulletin of Historical Research in Music Education* 8, no. 2 (July 1987): 63-82.

Schlenker, Alma. *Music in Bethlehem.* Bethlehem, PA: Oaks Printing Co., 1985.

Schnell, William Emmett. "The Choral Music of Johann Friedrich Peter (1746-1813)." DMA diss., University of Illinois, 1973.

Serwer, Howard. "Handel in Bethlehem." *Handel-Jahrbuch* 27 (1981): 107-16.

Sharp, Timothy W. "Moravian Choral Music." *The Choral Journal* 30, no. 3 (October 1989): 5-12.

Stillwell, Roy Edward. "Six Anthems by John Frederik Peter." DMA diss., University of Rochester, 1968.

Steelman, Robert, ed. *Catalog of the Lititz Congregation Collection.* Chapel Hill: University of North Carolina, 1981.

Strauss, Barbara Jo. "A Register of Music Performed in Concert, Nazareth, Pennsylvania, from 1796 to 1845: An Annotated Edition of an American Moravian Document." Master's thesis, University of Arizona, 1976.

Vogt, Peter. "A Bibliography of German Scholarship on Moravian Music." *Moravian Music Journal* 42, no. 2 (Fall 1997): 15-22.

Walters, Raymond. "Bach at Bethlehem, Pennsylvania." *Musical Quarterly* 21, no. 2 (April 1935): 179-89.

Williams, Henry L. "The Development of the Moravian Hymnal." *Transactions of the Moravian Historical Society* 18 (1962): 239-66.

Wolfe, Lucy Louise. "Moravian Church Music in Wachovia, North Carolina." SMM., Union Theological Seminary, 1951.

Chapter 5

Shape-Notes

Allison, Junius. "Orphan Character Notes in Appalachia." *North Carolina Folklore Journal* 32, no. 2 (1984): 82-90.

Anderson, Rick. "The Kentucky Harmonist: A Possible Source for Tunes Used in the Kentucky Revival, 1800-1805." Master's thesis, University of Cincinnati, 1994.

Bealle, John. *Public Worship, Private Faith: Sacred Harp and American Folksong.* Athens, GA: University of Georgia Press, 1997.

Bean, Shirley Ann. "The *Missouri Harmony*, 1820-1858: The Refinement of a Southern Tunebook." DMA diss., University of Missouri at Kansas City, 1973.

Beary, Shirley. "Stylistic Traits of Southern Shape-Note Gospel Songs." *Hymn* 30, no. 1 (January 1979): 26-33.

Brock, David A. "A Foundation for Defining Southern Shape-Note Folk Hymnody from 1800-1859 as a Learned Compositional Style." Ph.D. diss., Claremont Graduate School, 1996.

Card, Edith Bryson. "William Walker's Music Then and Now: A Study of Performance Style." Master's thesis, Florida State University, 1975.

Cobb, Buell E. *The Sacred Harp: A Tradition and Its Music.* Athens, GA: University of Georgia Press, 1989.

_____. "The Sacred Harp: An Overview of a Tradition." Master's thesis, Auburn University, 1969.

Cowell, S. R. "The Shaped-Note Singers and Their Music." *Score* (London) 12 (June 1955): 9-14.

Crouse, David L. "The Work of Allen D. Carden and Associates in the Shape-Note Tune-Books: *The Missouri Harmony, Western Harmony* and *United States Harmony.*" DMA thesis, Southern Baptist Theological Seminary, 1972.

Dyen, Doris J. "New Directions in Sacred Harp Singing." In *Folk and Modern Sound.* Jackson, MS: University of Mississippi, 1982.

_____. "The Role of Shape-Note Singing in the Musical Culture of Black Communities in Southeast Alabama." Ph.D. diss, University of Illinois at Urbana-Champaign, 1977.

_____. "Shape-Note Singing Traditions." In *Musical Roots of the South.* Atlanta: Southern Arts Federation, 1991.

Ellington, Charles Linwood. "The Sacred Harp Tradition of the South: Its Origin and Evolution." Ph.D. diss., Florida State University, 1969.

Eskew, Harry. "Christian Harmony Singing in Alabama: Its Adaptation and Survival." *Inter-American Music Review* 10, no. 2 (Spring-Summer 1989): 169-75.

_____. "Shape-Note Hymnody in the Shenandoah Valley, 1816-1860." Ph.D. diss., Tulane University, 1966.

_____. "Using Early American Hymnals and Tunebooks." *Notes* 27, no. 1 (September 1970): 19-23.

_____. "William Walker and His Southern Harmony." *Baptist History and Heritage* 21, no. 4 (1986): 19-26.

Hall, James W. "The Tune-Book in American Culture, 1800-1820." Ph.D. diss., University of Pennsylvania, 1967.

Hall, Paul M. "The *Musical Million*: A Study and Analysis of the Periodical Promoting Music Reading through Shape-Notes in North America from 1870-1914." DMA diss., Catholic University of America, 1970.

_____. "The Shape-Note Hymnals and Tune Books of Ruebush-Kieffer Company." *Hymn* 22, no. 3 (July 1971): 69-76.

Hammond, Paul. "Jesse B. Aikin and The Christian Minstrel." *American Music* 3, no. 4 (1985): 442-51.

Hinton, Sam. "The Shape-Note Hymns: An American Choral Tradition." *The Choral Journal* 13, no. 5 (1973): 7-11.

Jackson, George Pullen. *The Story of the Sacred Harp, 1844-1944.* Nashville: Vanderbilt University Press, 1944.

Jensen, David G., comp. *An American Folk-Hymn Index of Seven Shape-Note Hymnals*. Portland, OR: the author, 1993.

Kelton, Mai Hogan. "Analysis of the Music Curriculum of the Sacred Harp (American Tune-Book, 1971 edition) and Its Continuing Traditions." Ph.D. diss., University of Alabama, 1985.

Lazenby, Jimmy Ray. "The Characteristics of Sacred Harp Music: The Problem of Maintaining the Style of Music in Composition and Arrangements." Master's thesis, Stephen F. Austin State University, 1972.

Loftis, Deborah Carlton. "Big Singing Day in Benton, Kentucky: A Study of the History, Ethnic Identity, and Musical Style of Southern Harmony Singers." Ph.D. diss., University of Kentucky, 1987.

_____. "Southern Harmony Singing: A Tradition of Shape-Note Practice." *Performance Practice Review* 3, no. 2 (Fall 1990): 165-69.

Logsdon, Guy. "Fa-sol-la (Shape-Note) Singing." In *Festival of American Folklife*. Washington, DC: Smithsonian Institution, 1982.

Lowens, Irving. "Tune Books, Tunesmiths and Singing Schools." *Etude* 74 (November 1956): 20+.

_____. "Shape-Notes, New England Music, and White Spirituals." Parts 1 and 2. *Etude* 76 (January 1957): 15-64; (February 1957): 20+.

Lowens, Irving, and Allen Perdue Britton. *The Easy Instructor, 1798-1931: A History and Bibliography of the First Shape Note Tune Book*. Ann Arbor, MI: N.p., 1953.

McGill, Lynn D. "A Study of Shape-Note Music as a Resource and as a System of Teaching Music." Master's thesis, University of Tennessee, 1968.

McKenzie, Wallace. "The Alto Parts in the 'True Dispersed Harmony' of the Sacred Harp Revisions." *Musical Quarterly* 73, no. 2 (1989): 153-71.

_____. "Anthems of the Sacred Harp Tunesmiths." *American Music* 9, no. 3 (Fall 1988): 247-63.

Miller, Terry E. "Alexander Auld and American Shape-Note Music." Master's thesis, Indiana University, 1971.

_____. "Old Time Shape-Note Singing Schools in Eastern Kentucky." *Southern Quarterly* 20, no. 1 (Fall 1981): 35-45.

_____. "Voices from the Past: The Singing and the Preaching at Otter Creek Church." *Journal of American Folklore* 88, no. 349 (July-September 1975): 266-82.

Mitchell, Henry Chesterfield. "The 'Sacred Harp' Singing Group as an Instance of Non-Formal Education." Ph.D. diss., Florida State University, 1976.

Moser, M. Y. "Christian Harmony Singing at Etowah." *Appalachian Journal* 1, no. 4 (1974): 263-70.

Music, David W. "Alexander Johnson and the Tennessee Harmony." *Current Musicology* 37-38 (1984): 59-73.

_____. "Ananias Davisson, Robert Boyd, Reubin Monday, John Martin and Archibald Rhea in East Tennessee, 1816-26." *American Music* 1, no. 3 (Fall 1983): 72-84.

_____. "The Anthem in Southern Four-Shape Shape-Note Tunebooks, 1816-1860." In *American Musical Life in Context and Practice to 1865*, ed. James R. Heintze. New York: Garland, 1994.

O'Brien, James Patrick. "An Experimental Study of the Use of Shape Notes in Developing Sight Singing." Ph.D. diss., University of Colorado at Boulder, 1969.

Oswalt, Lewis Earl. "Rigdon McCoy McIntosh: Teacher, Composer, Editor, and Publisher." DMA diss., New Orleans Baptist Theological Seminary, 1991.

Patterson, Daniel W. Introduction to *The Social Harp*. Athens, GA: University of Georgia Press, 1973.

_____. "William Hauser's Hesperial Harp and Olive Leaf: Shape-Note Tunebooks as Emblems of Change and Progress." *Journal of American Folklore* 101, no. 399 (January-March 1988): 23-36.

Richardson, Thomas. "Daddy's Shaped Notes: A Review of Sacred Harp Traditions." *Mississippi Folklore Register* 13 (Spring 1979): 45-51.

Scott, Joseph Dennie. "The Tunebooks of William Hauser." DMA diss., New Orleans Baptist Theological Seminary, 1987.

Stanislaw, Richard J. *A Checklist of Four-Shape Shape-Note Tunebooks*. Brooklyn, NY: Institute for Studies in American Music, Brooklyn College, 1978.

_____. "Choral Performance Practice in the Four-Shape Literature of American Frontier Singing Schools." Ph.D. diss., University of Illinois at Urbana-Champaign, 1976.

Stanley, David H. "The Gospel-Singing Convention in South Georgia." *Journal of American Folklore* 95, no. 275 (January-March 1982): 1-32.

Steel, David Warren. "John Wyeth and the Development of Southern Folk Hymnody." In *Music from the Middle Ages through the Twentieth Century: Essays in Honor of Gwynn S. McPeek.* New York: Gordon and Breach, 1988.

_____. "Lazarus J. Jones and the Southern Minstrel (1849)." *American Music* 36, no. 2 (1988): 123-57.

_____. "Stephen Jenks (1772-1856): American Composer and Tunebook Compiler." Ph.D. diss., University of Michigan, 1982.

_____. "Truman S. Wetmore of Winchester and His Republican Harmony." *Connecticut Historical Society Bulletin* 45, no. 3 (July 1980): 75-89.

Stegall, Joel R. "Shape-Notes and Choral Singing: Did We Throw Out the Baby with the Bath Water?" *The Choral Journal* 19, no. 2 (October 1978): 5-10.

Sutton, Brett. "Shape-Note Tunebooks and Primitive Hymns." *Ethnomusicology* 26, no. 1 (January 1982): 11-26.

Tadlock, Paula. "Shape-Note Singing in Mississippi." In *Discourse in Ethnomusicology: Essays in Honor of George List,* ed. Caroline Card and others. Bloomington, IN: Indiana University, 1978.

Talmadge, William. "Folk Organum: A Study of Origins." *American Music* 2, no. 3 (Fall 1984): 47-65.

Warren, James Sullivan, Jr. *Warren's Minstrel [1856].* Athens, OH: Ohio University, 1984.

Young, J. Bradford. "Shape-Note Tunebooks in the Deep South." *Popular Music and Society* 10, no 3 (1986): 17-27.

Chapter 6

African-American Music

Anderson, Talmadge, ed. *Black Studies: Theory, Method, and Cultural Perspectives.* Pullman, WA: Washington State University, 1990.

Anderson, Toni Passmore. "The Fisk Jubilee Singers: Performing Ambassadors for the Survival of an American Treasure, 1871-1878." Ph.D. diss., Georgia State University, 1997.

Armetta, Anne Reisner. "Aspects of Musical Experience of African-American and Mexican-American Choral Ensembles with Implications for Choral Music Education." Ph.D. diss., Northwestern University, 1994.

Ballou, Leonard R. "Negroes and Music in Nineteenth-Century America: A Survey." Master's thesis, Virginia State College, 1964.

Baraka, Imamu Amiri. *Black Music.* New York: W. Morrow, 1971.

Bennett, Carolyn L. "African Survivals in the Religious Music Tradition of the United States Negro." Master's thesis, DePaul University, 1968.

Boyer, H. C. "Tracking the Tradition: New Orleans Sacred Music." *Black Music Research Journal* 8, no. 1 (1988): 135-47.

Blackwell, Lois S. *The Wings of the Dove: The Story of Gospel Music in America.* Norfolk, VA: Donning, 1978.

Brooks, Tilford. *America's Black Musical Heritage.* Englewood Cliffs, NJ: Prentice-Hall, 1984.

Broughton, Viv. *Black Gospel: An Illustrated History of the Gospel Sound.* New York: Sterling Publishing Co., 1985. Poole, Dorset; Blandford Press.

Burnim, Mellonee Victoria. "The Black Gospel Music Tradition: Symbol of Ethnicity." Ph.D. diss., Indiana University, 1980.

Cogdell, Jacqueline Delores. "An Analytical Study of the Similarities and Differences in the American Black Spiritual and Gospel Song from the South-East Region of Georgia." Master's thesis, University of California at Los Angeles, 1972.

Cohen, Norm, and Paul Wells. *See chapter 1.*

Courlander, Harold. *Negro Folk Music, USA.* New York: Dover, 1992.

Crawford, Richard. "On Two Traditions of Black Music Research." *Black Music Research Journal* 1, no. 1 (1986): 1-9.

Cusic, Don. *The Sound of Light: A History of Gospel Music.* Bowling Green, OH: Bowling Green State University Popular Press, 1990.

De Lerma, Dominique-René. *Bibliography of Black Music.* 4 vols. Westport, CT: Greenwood, 1981-84.

_____. *Reflections on Afro-American Music.* With contributions from Richard L. Abrams and others. Kent, OH: Kent State University Press, 1973.

_____. "A Selective List of Choral Music by Black Composers." *The Choral Journal* 12, no. 8 (April 1972): 5-6.

Djedje, J. C. "Gospel Music in the Los Angeles Black Community: A Historical Overview." *Black Music Research Journal* 9, no. 1 (1989): 35-79.

DuPree, Sherry Sherrod, and Herbert C. DuPree. *African-American Good News (Gospel) Music.* Washington, DC: Middle Atlantic Regional Press, 1993.

Dyen, Doris Jane. "The Role of Shape-Note Singing in the Musical Culture of Black Communities in Southeast Alabama." Ph.D. diss., University of Illinois at Urbana-Champaign, 1977.

Floyd, Samuel A., Jr. *The Power of Black Music: Interpreting Its History from Africa to the United States.* New York: Oxford University Press, 1995.

Floyd, Samuel A., Jr., and Marsha J. Reisser. *Black Music Biography: An Annotated Bibliography.* White Plains, NY: Kraus International Publications, 1987.

_____. *Black Music in the United States: An Annotated Bibliography of Selected Reference and Research Materials.* Millwood, NY and London: Kraus International Publications, 1983.

Garcia, W. B. "Church Music by Black Composers: A Bibliography of Choral Music." *Black Perspectives in Music* 2, no. 2 (Fall 1974): 145-57.

George, Zelma Watson. "A Guide to Negro Music: An Annotated Bibliography of Negro Folk Music and Art Music by Negro Composers or Based on Negro Thematic Material." Ed.D. diss., New York University, 1954.

Green, Mildred Denby. *Black Women Composers: A Genesis*. Boston: Twayne, 1983.

Haas, Robert B., ed. *William Grant Still and the Fusion of Cultures in American Music*. Los Angeles: Black Sparrow Press, 1972.

Hare, Maud. *Negro Musicians and Their Music*. Washington, DC: The Associated Publishers, Inc., [1936].

Harris, Carl Gordon, Jr. "A Study of Characteristic Stylistic Trends Found in the Choral Works of a Selected Group of Afro-American Composers and Arrangers." DMA diss., University of Missouri, 1972.

Harris, Robert A. "African Retentions in American Vocal and Choral Music." In *Black Studies: Theory, Method, and Cultural Perspectives*. Pullman, WA: Washington State University, 1990.

Hayes, Stephen L. "The Philander Smith College 'Collegiate' Choir: An African-American Choral Tradition." *Western Journal of Black Studies* 16, no. 4 (1992): 205-206.

Hinson, Glen Douglas. "When the Words Roll and the Fire Flows: Spirit, Style and Experience in African-American Gospel Performance." Ph.D. diss., University of Pennsylvania, 1989.

Hygh, Haywood, Jr. "The Fisk Jubilee Singers." *The Choral Journal* 12 (November 1971): 18.

Jackson, Irene V., comp. *Afro-American Religious Music: A Bibliography and a Catalogue of Gospel Music*. Westport, CT: Greenwood Press, 1979.

_____. "Afro-American Gospel Music and Its Social Setting with Special Attention to Roberta Martin." Ph.D. diss., Wesleyan University, 1974.

Jackson-Brown, Irene. "Developments in Black Gospel Performance and Scholarship." *Black Music Research Journal* 10, no. 1 (1990): 36-42.

Johnson, Grace Gray. "Choral Organizations in Selected Negro Institutions of Higher Education." Master's thesis, Boston University, 1964.

Johnson, James P. *Bibliographic Guide to the Study of Afro-American Music*. Washington: Howard University Libraries, 1973.

Katz, Bernard, ed. *The Social Implications of Early Negro Music in the United States*. New York: Arno Press, 1969.

Keck, George R., and Sherrill V. Martin, eds. *Feel the Spirit: Studies in Nineteenth-Century Afro-American Music*. New York: Greenwood Press, 1988.

Kinchen, James Benjamin, Jr. "Black Gospel Music and Its Impact on Traditional Choral Singing at Historically Black Institutions of Higher Learning." *The Choral Journal* 27, no. 1 (August 1986): 11-19.

Lau, Barbara A. "Religious Rituals and Cultural Cohesion—A Case Study: Shape-Note Singing by Urban Black Americans in Four Midwestern Cities." *Mid-American Folklore* 10, no. 2-3 (Fall-Winter 1982): 27-57.

Lawrenz, Marguerite Martha. *Bibliography and Index of Negro Music*. Detroit: Board of Education, 1968.

Lyle-Smith, Eva Diane. "Nathaniel Clark Smith (1877-1934): African American Musician, Music Educator and Composer." Ph.D. diss., University of North Texas, 1993.

McBrier, Vivian Flagg. "The Life and Works of Robert Nathaniel Dett." Ph.D. diss., Catholic University of America, 1967.

McCarroll, Jesse Cornelius. "Black Influence on Southern White Protestant Church Music during Slavery." Ph.D. diss., Columbia University, 1972.

Marsh, J. B. T. *The Story of the Jubilee Singers: With Their Songs*. 1880. Reprint, New York: AMS Press, [1971]. This work exists in many reprints.

Maultsby, Portia Katerina. "Afro-American Religious Music: 1619-1861." Ph.D. diss., University of Wisconsin at Madison, 1974.

_____. "Afro-American Religious Music: A Study in Diversity." Papers of the Hymn Society of America, vol. 35. Springfield, OH: Hymn Society of America, [1981].

Meadows, Eddie S. *Theses and Dissertations on Black American Music*. Beverly Hills, CA: T. Front Musical Literature, 1980.

Murphy, J. R. "The Survival of African Music in America." *Popular Science Monthly* 55 (September 1899): 660-72.

Newman, Richard. *Black Access: A Bibliography of Afro-American Bibliographies*. Westport, CT: Greenwood Press, 1984.

Norris, Ethel Maureen. "Music in the Black and White Communities in Petersburg, Virginia, 1865-1900." Ph.D. diss., Ohio State University, 1994.

Peek, Philip M., comp. *Catalog of Afro-American Music and Oral Data Holdings*. Indiana University Archives of Traditional Music. Bloomington, IN: Indiana University, 1970.

Pike, Gustavus D. *The Jubilee Singers and Their Campaign for Twenty Thousand Dollars*. 1873. Reprint, New York: AMS Press, 1974.

Raichelson, Richard M. "Black Religious Folksong: A Study in Generic and Social Change." Ph.D. diss., University of Pennsylvania, 1975.

Ricks, George Robinson. *Some Aspects of the Religious Music of the United States Negro: An Ethnomusicological Study with Special Emphasis on the Gospel Tradition*. New York: Arno Press, 1977.

Roach, Hildred. *Black American Music: Past and Present*. 2nd ed. Reissue, with minor corrections and updating. Malabar, FL: Krieger Publishing, 1994.

Ryder, George Atkins. "Melodic and Rhythmic Elements of American Negro Folk Songs as Employed in Cantatas by Selected American Composers between 1932 and 1967." Ph.D. diss., New York University, 1970.

Silveri, Louis D. "The Singing Tour of the Fisk Jubilee Singers, 1871-1874." In *Feel the Spirit: Studies in Nineteenth-Century Afro-American Music*, ed. George R. Keck and Sherrill V. Martin. New York: Greenwood Press, 1988.

Skowronski, JoAnn. *Black Music in America: A Bibliography*. Metuchen, NJ: Scarecrow Press, 1981.

Smith, Vernon Leon. "The Hampton Institute Choir, 1873-1973 (Virginia)." Ph.D. diss., Florida State University, 1985.

Southern, Eileen. *The Music of Black Americans: A History*. 3rd ed. New York: W. W. Norton, 1997.

_____. *Readings in Black American Music*. 2nd ed. New York: W. W. Norton, 1983.

Southern, Eileen, and Josephine Wright. *African-American Traditions in Songs, Sermon, Tale, and Dance, 1600-1920: An Annotated Bibliography of Literature, Collections, and Artworks.* New York: Greenwood Press, 1990.

Spencer, Jon Michael. *Black Hymnody: A Hymnological History of the African-American Church.* Knoxville, TN: University of Tennessee, 1992.

———. "The Hymnody of Black Methodists." *Theology Today* 46 (1990): 373-85.

———. *Protest & Praise: Sacred Music of Black Religion.* Minneapolis: Fortress Press, 1990.

———. *Re-Searching Black Music.* Knoxville, TN: University of Tennessee Press, 1996.

Spottswood, Richard K. *See also chapter 1.*

Spradling, Mary Mace. *In Black and White: A Guide to Magazine Articles, Newspaper Articles, and Books Concerning More Than 15,000 Black Individuals and Groups.* Detroit: Gale Publishers, 1980.

Taylor, Jewel Annabell. *Technical Practices of Negro Composers in Choral Works for A Capella Choir.* Imprint. Eastman School of Music Archives, Rochester, NY, 1960.

Trice, Patricia J. *Choral Arrangements of the African-American Spirituals: Historical Overview and Annotated Listings.* Westport, CT: Greenwood Press, 1998.

———. "Unaccompanied Choral Arrangements of African-American Spirituals: The 'Signifying' Tradition Continues." *The Choral Journal* 34, no. 7 (February 1994): 15-21.

Trotter, James M. *Music and Some Highly Musical People.* Chicago: Afro-American Press, 1969.

West, Earle H. *A Bibliography of Doctoral Research on the Negro, 1933-1966.* Ann Arbor: University Microfilms, 1969.

White, Evelyn Davidson. *Choral Music by African-American Composers: A Selected, Annotated Bibliography.* 2nd ed. Lanham, MD: Scarecrow Press, 1996.

White, Newman L. *American Negro Folk-Songs.* Cambridge: Harvard University Press, 1928.

Williams, Ethel L., and Clinton F. Brown. *Afro-American Religious Studies: A Comprehensive Bibliography with Locations in American Libraries.* Metuchen, NJ: Scarecrow Press, 1972.

Williams-Jones, Pearl. "Structure and Spirit: Improvisation Qualities of Black American Gospel Songs and Sermons." Conference proceedings, Symposium of Improvisation in the Performing Arts. Honolulu, HI, 1983.

Wright, Josephine, and Samuel A. Floyd, Jr., eds. *New Perspectives on Music: Essays in Honor of Eileen Southern.* Warren, MI: Harmonie Park Press, 1992.

Yizar, Terrye Barron. "Afro-American Music in North America before 1865: A Study of 'The First of August Celebration' in the United States." Ph.D. diss., University of California at Berkeley, 1984.

Chapter 7

Slave Songs and Spirituals

Allen, William Francis, Charles Ware, and Lucy McKim Garrison. *Slave Songs of the United States.* 1867. Reprint, with an introduction by William K. McNeil, Freeport, NY: Books for Libraries Press, 1971.

Anderson, Margaret Bassett. "The Treatment of Some of the Bible Stories in Negro Spirituals." Master's thesis, Columbia University, 1930.

Backus, E. M. "Negro Hymns from Georgia." *Journal of the American Folklore Society* 10 (1897): 202; 11 (1898): 22.

_____. "Negro Songs from North Carolina." *Journal of the American Folklore Society* 11 (1898): 60.

Barton, William Eleazar. *Old Plantation Hymns.* 1899. Reprint, New York: AMS Press, [1972].

_____. "Hymns of the Negro." *New England Magazine* 19 (January 1899): 609-24.

Burnim, Mellonee Victoria. "The Black Gospel Music Tradition: Symbol of Ethnicity." Ph.D. diss., Indiana University, 1980.

Burns, Pamela Teresa. "The Negro Spiritual: From the Southern Plantations to the Concert Stages of America." DMA diss., University of Alabama, 1993.

_____. "The Negro Spiritual: Its Origin and Musical Aspects in Relation to Performance." Master's thesis, Southern Illinois University at Carbondale, 1989.

Burton, William. "The History of the Negro Spiritual and Its Contribution to Sacred Music." Master's thesis, San Francisco Theological Seminary, 1943.

Carter, Marva Griffin. "Hall Johnson (1888-1970): Preserver of the Old Negro Spiritual." Master's thesis, Boston University, 1975.

Cleveland Public Library. *Index to Negro Spirituals*. Cleveland, OH: Cleveland Public Library, 1937.

Cone, James H. *The Spiritual and the Blues: An Interpretation*. New York: The Seabury Press, 1972.

Crutchfield, Mary Elizabeth. "The White Spiritual." Master's thesis, Union Theological Seminary, 1946.

Dixon, Christa K. *Negro Spirituals: From Bible to Folksong*. Philadelphia: Fortress Press, 1976.

Djedje, Jacqueline Cogdell. *American Black Spiritual and Gospel Songs from Southeast Georgia: A Comparative Study*. Los Angeles: University of California Center for Afro-American Studies, 1978.

Dyen, Doris Jane. *See chapter 5*.

Epstein, Dena J. "Black Spirituals: Their Emergence into Public Knowledge." *Black Music Research Journal* 10, no. 1 (Spring 1990): 58-66.

_____. *Sinful Tunes and Spirituals: Black Folk Music to the Civil War*. Urbana, IL: University of Illinois Press, 1977.

_____. "Slave Music in the United States before 1860: A Survey of Sources." Parts 1 and 2. *Notes* 20 (Spring-Summer 1963): 195-212, 377-90.

_____. "A White Origin for the Black Spiritual? An Invalid Theory and How It Grew." *American Music* 1, no. 2 (Summer 1983): 53-59.

Evans, Arthur Lee. "The Development of the Negro Spiritual as Choral Art Music by Afro-American Composers with an Annotated Guide to the Performance of Selected Spirituals." Ph.D. diss., University of Miami, 1972.

Fisher, Miles Mark. *Negro Slave Songs in the United States*. New York: Citadel Press, 1969.

Griffin, G. H. "Slave Music of the South." *American Missionary* 36 (1882): 70-72.

Harris, Carl, Jr. "The Negro Spiritual: Stylistic Developments through Performance Practices." *The Choral Journal* 14 (1973): 15.

Haskell, M. A. "Negro Spirituals." *Century Magazine* 58 (1899): 577-81.

Higginson, T. W. "Negro Spirituals." *Atlantic Monthly* 19 (1867): 385-694.

Hough, Robin. "Choirs of Angels Armed for War: Reverend Marshall W. Taylor's 'A collection of Revival Hymns and Plantation Melodies.'" In *Feel the Spirit: Studies in Nineteenth-Century Afro-American Music*, ed. George R. Keck and Sherrill V. Martin. New York: Greenwood Press, 1988.

Hughes, Langston. "Negro Expressions: Spirituals, Seculars, Ballads and Work Songs." In *The Making of Black America: Essays in Negro Life and History*. Vol. 2. New York: Atheneum, 1969.

Hulan, Richard Huffman. "Camp Meeting Spiritual Folk Songs: Legacy of the 'Great Revival in the West.'" Ph.D. diss., University of Texas at Austin, 1978.

Jackson, George Pullen. "The Genesis of the Negro Spiritual." *The American Mercury* 26 (1932): 243-55.

_____. *White and Negro Spirituals, Their Life Span and Kinship, Tracing 200 Years of Untrammeled Song Making and Singing among Our Country Folk, with 116 Songs as Sung by Both Races*. 1943. Reprint, New York: Da Capo Press, 1975.

_____. *White Spirituals in the Southern Uplands: The Story of the Fasola Folk, Their Songs, Singings, and "Buckwheat Notes."* 1933. Reprint, New York: Dover Publications, 1965.

Jackson-Brown, Irene V. "Afro-American Sacred Song in the Nineteenth Century: A survey of a Neglected Source. *The Black Perspective in Music* 4 (1976): 22-38.

Johnson, Guy B. "The Negro Spiritual, a Problem in Anthropology." *American Anthropologist* 33 (1931): 157-71.

"Jubilee Singers." *American Missionary* 34 (1880): 291.

Lehmann, Theo. *Negro Spirituals: Geschichte und Theologie*. Berlin: Eckhart, 1965.

Levine, Lawrence. "Slave Songs and Slave Consciousness: An Exploration in Neglected Sources." In *Anonymous American: Explorations in Nineteenth-Century Social History*. Englewood Cliffs, NJ: Prentice-Hall, 1971.

"Literature of the Day: Slave Songs of the United States." *Lippincott's Magazine* 2 (March 1868): 617-19.

Long, Norman G. "The Theology and Psychology of the Negro's Religion prior to 1860 as Shown Particularly in the Spiritual." Master's thesis, 1956, Oberlin University.

Lord, Donald. "The Slave Song as a Historical Source." *Social Education* 35, no. 7 (November 1971): 763-76, 821.

Lorenz, Ellen Jane. *Glory, Hallelujah! The Story of the Campmeeting Spiritual.* Nashville, TN: Abingdon Press, 1980.

Lovell, John. Black Song: *The Forge and the Flame: The Story of How the Afro-American Spiritual Was Hammered Out.* 1972. Reprint, New York: Schirmer Books, 1980.

McLaughlin,Wayne B. "Symbolism and Mysticism in the Spiritual." *Phylon* 24 (1963): 69-77.

Maultsby, Portia Katerina. "Afro-American Religious Music: 1619-1861. Part I-Historical Development. Part II-Computer Analysis of One Hundred Spirituals." Ph.D. diss., University of Wisconsin at Madison, 1974.

_____. "Black Spirituals: An Analysis of Textual Forms and Structures." *The Black Perspective in Music* 4, no. 1 (Spring 1976): 54-69.

Murray, Charlotte. "The Story of Harry T. Burleigh." *The Hymn* 17, no. 4 (1966): 101-11.

Parrish, Lydia, comp. *Slave Songs of the Georgia Sea Islands.* Athens, GA: University of Georgia, 1992.

Patterson, Daniel W. "Folk-Song Elements in the Shaker Spiritual." Master's thesis, University of North Carolina at Chapel Hill, 1955.

_____. "Hunting for the American White Spiritual: A Survey of Scholarship, with Discography." *ARSC Journal* 3, no. 1 (Winter 1970-71): 7-18.

Pinkston, Alfred Adolphus. "Lined Hymns, Spirituals, and the Associated Lifestyle of Rural Black People in the United States." Ph.D. diss., University of Miami, 1975.

Proctor, Henry Hugh. "The Theology of the Songs of the Southern Slave (1907)." *The Journal of Black Sacred Music* 2, no. 1 (Spring 1988): 51-64.

Ricks, George Robinson. *Some Aspects of the Religious Music of the United States Negro: An Ehtnomusicological Study with Special Emphasis on the Gospel Tradition.* New York: Arno Press, 1977.

Ryder, C. J. "The Theology of Plantation Songs." *American Missionary* 45 (1891): 123-24; 46 (1892): 9-16.

Shirley, Wayne. "The Coming of 'Deep River.'" *American Music* 15, no. 4 (Winter 1997): 493-534.

Simpson, Anne Key. *Hard Trials: The Life and Music of Harry T. Burleigh.* Metuchen, NJ: Scarecrow Press, 1990. Composers of North America. No. 8.

Southall, Geneva H. "Black Composers and Religious Music." *The Black Perspective in Music* 2, no. 1 (Spring 1974): 45-50.

Southern, Eileen. "An Origin for the Negro Spiritual." In *The Theatre of Black Americans: A Collection of Critical Essays,* ed. Errol Hill. New York: Applause Press, 1983.

Trice, Patricia J. *Choral Arrangements of the African-American Spirituals: Historical Overview and Annotated Listings.* Westport, CT: Greenwood Press, 1998.

_____. "Unaccompanied Choral Arrangements of African-American Spirituals: The 'Signifying' Tradition Continues." *The Choral Journal* 34, no. 7 (February 1994): 15-21.

Walker, Wyatt Tee. "The Soulful Journey of the Negro Spiritual." *Negro Digest* 12 (1963): 83-95.

Whalum, Wendell P. "The Spiritual as Mature Choral Composition." *Black World* 23 (1974): 34-39.

Winans, Robert. "Saddy Night and Sunday Too: The Uses of Slave Songs in the WPA Ex-Slave Narratives for Historical Study." *New Jersey Folklife* 7 (1982): 10-15.

Work, John W. *American Negro Songs and Spirituals.* New York: Bonanza Books, 1960.

Chapter 8

Music Education and Pedagogy

Armetta, Anne Reisner. *See chapter 6.*

Blum, Beula Eisenstadt. "Solmization in Nineteenth-Century American Sight-Singing Instruction." Ph.D. diss., University of Maryland, 1968.

The Commencement, Progress and Results of Systematic Instruction in Music in the Primary Schools of Boston. Boston: J. F. Loughlin, 1974. Microfilm.

Dox, Thurston J. "George Frederick Bristow and the New York Public Schools." *American Music* 9, no. 4 (Winter 1991): 339-52.

Eaklor, Vicki. "Roots of an Ambivalent Culture: Music Education, and Music Education in Antebellum America." *Journal of Research in Music Education* 33, no. 2 (Summer 1985): 87-99.

Fisher, Robert. "H. Theodore Hach and *The Musical Magazine*: A Historical Perspective." *Council for Research in Music Education Bulletin* 92 (Summer 1987): 35-46.

Fouts, Gordon. "Music Instruction in America to around 1830 as Suggested by the Hartzler Collection of Early Protestant American Tune Books." Ph.D. diss., University of Iowa, 1968.

Larson, William S. *Bibliography of Research Studies in Music Education, 1932-1948.* Chicago: MENC, 1949. Supplement for 1949-56 in the *Journal for Research in Music Education* 5 (1957):

63-225. Roderick D. Gordon published the supplements for 1957-63, now entitled "Doctoral Dissertations in Music and Music Education," in vol. 12 (1964): 2-122; for 1963-67 in vol. 16 (1968): 87-216; for 1968-71 in vol. 20 (1972): 2-185; for 1972-77, in vol. 26 (1978): 135-415.

Mason, Lowell. *A Glance at Pestalozzianism.* New York: Mason Brothers, 1863.

_____. *How Shall I Teach? or Hints to Teachers as to the Use of Music and Its Notation.* New York: Mason Brothers, 1860.

_____. *Manual of the Boston Academy of Music for Instruction in the Elements of Vocal Music: On the System of Pestalozzi.* Boston: Wilkins, Carter, 1848.

Mason, Luther Whiting. *First Music Reader: A Course of Exercises in the Elements of Vocal Music and Sight-Singing, with Choice Rote Songs for the Use of the Youngest Pupils in Schools and Families.* Boston: Ginn, 1872.

_____. *The National Music Teacher: A Practical Guide in Teaching Vocal Music and Sight-Singing to the Youngest Pupils in Schools and Families; Designed to Accompany the National Music Charts and Music Readers.* Boston: Ginn Brothers, 1872.

Miller, David Michael. "The Beginnings of Music in the Boston Public Schools: Decisions of the Boston School Committee in 1837 and 1845 in Light of Religious and Moral Concerns of the Time." Ph.D. diss., University of North Texas, 1989.

Muradian, Thaddeus George. *See chapter 14.*

Parker, Harlan D. "The Musical Cabinet: An Educational Journal of the Boston Area in the 1840s." *Bulletin of the Council for Research in Music Education* 116 (Spring 1993): 51-60.

Plum, Nancy. "Innovation in Choral Music Education: Against the Odds." *The Sonneck Society for American Music Bulletin* 19, no. 3 (Fall 1993): 13-14.

Pokorny, Mary Heliodore. "Lowell Mason's Contribution to the Field of Music Education in America." Master's thesis, DePaul University, 1952.

Root, George F. *The Normal Musical Hand-Book: A Book of Instruction and Reference for Teachers of Notation, Voice Culture, Harmony and Church Music, in Classes.* Cincinnati: J. Church, 1872.

Scanlon, Mary Browning. "Lowell Mason in Music Education." Master's thesis, Eastman School of Music, University of Rochester, 1940.

_____. "Lowell Mason's Philosophy of Music Education." *Music Educators Journal* 28 (January 1942): 24-25, 70.

Small, Arnold M. *Bibliography of Research Studies in Music Education, 1932-1944.* Iowa City: State University of Iowa Press [1944].

Smith, Charles Kenneth. "Choral Music Education as Aesthetic Education." Ph.D. diss., Arizona State University, 1974.

Tufts, Rosanna. "The Life and Works of John Wheller Tufts." Master's thesis, Peabody Institute of the Johns Hopkins University, 1985.

White, J. Perry. "Entertainment, Enlightenment, and Service: A History and Description of Choral Music in Higher Education." *College Music Symposium* 23, no. 2 (Fall 1983): 10-20.

Chapter 9

Composers and Conductors

These entries are arranged by composer or musician.

Bliss, Philip P. Neil, Bobby Joe. "Philip P. Bliss (1838-1876): Gospel Hymn Composer and Compiler." Ed.D. diss., New Orleans Baptist Theological Seminary, 1977.

_____. Smucker, David Joseph. "Philip Paul Bliss and the Musical, Cultural and Religious Sources of the Gospel Music Tradition in the United States, 1850-1876." Ph.D. diss., Boston University, 1981.

_____. Whittle, D. W., ed. *Memoirs of Philip P. Bliss.* New York: Barnes, 1877.

Bradbury, William B. Stevenson, R. "William Batchelder Bradbury in Europe, 1847-1849." *Inter-American Music Review* 2, no. 1 (1979): 41-44.

_____. Wingard, Alan Burl. "The Life and Works of William Batchelder Bradbury, 1816-1868." DMA diss., Southern Baptist Theological Seminary, 1973.

Bristow, George. Rogers, Delmer, D. "Nineteenth-Century Music in New York City as Reflected in the Career of George Frederick Bristow." Ph.D. diss., University of Michigan, 1967.

_____. Yellin, Victor Fell. "Bristow's Divorce." *American Music* 12, no. 3 (Fall 1994): 229-54.

Carr, Benjamin. Keenan, Joseph John. "The Catholic Church Music of Benjamin Carr." Master's thesis, Catholic University of America, 1970.

_____. Sieck, Stephen. "Musical Tastes in Post-Revolutionary America as Seen through Carr's Musical Journal for the Piano Forte." Ph.D. diss., University of Cincinnati, 1991.

_____. Smith, Ronnie L. "The Church Music of Benjamin Carr (1768-1831). DMA. diss., Southwestern Baptist Theological Seminary, 1969.

_____. Sprenkle, C. A. "The Life and Works of Benjamin Carr." Ph.D. diss., Peabody Conservatory, 1970.

Christiansen, F. Melius. Hanson, Richard David. "An Analysis of Selected Choral Works of F. Melius Christiansen." Ph.D. diss., University of Illinois at Urbana-Champaign, 1970.

_____. Johnson, Albert Rykken. "The Christiansen Choral Tradition: F. Melius Christiansen, Olaf C. Christiansen, and Paul J. Christiansen." Ph. D. diss., University of Iowa, 1973.

_____. Nelson, Leola M. "F. Melius Christiansen: Study of His Life and Work as a Norwegian-American Contribution to American Culture." Ph.D. diss., University of Iowa, 1943.

Damrosch, Walter. Perryman, William Ray. "Walter Damrosch: An Educational Force in American Music." Ph.D. diss., Indiana University, 1972.

Douglas, Charles Winfred. Douglas, Anne Woodward, and Leonard Ellinwood. *The Life and Work of Charles Winfred Douglas.* New York: Hymn Society of America, 1975.

Duss, John S. Pope, Mary Bhame. "The Sacred Choral Works of John S. Duss." Master's thesis, Southern Baptist Theological Seminary, 1971.

Dvorak, Antonin. Strimple, Nick. "The Choral Works: Te Deum and The American Flag." In *Dvorak in America: 1892-1894.* Portland: Amadeus, 1993.

Foerster, Adolph M. Park, Michung. "Adolph Martin Foerster: His Life and Music." DMA diss., The Johns Hopkins University, 1996.

Fry, William Henry. Kauffman, Byron Forrest. "Choral Works of William Henry Fry." DMA diss., University of Illinois, 1975.

_____. Upton, William Treat. *William Henry Fry, American Journalist and Composer-Critic.* 1954. Reprint, New York: Da Capo Press, 1974.

Gould, Nathaniel Duren. Ingalls, Janyce Greenleaf. "Nathaniel Duren Gould, 1781-1864." Master's thesis, University of Lowell, 1980.

Hadley, Henry. Berthoud, Paul P. *The Musical Works of Dr. Henry Hadley, Compiled and Listed in Two Parts.* New York: The National Association for American Composers and Conductors and the Henry Hadley Foundation, 1942.

_____. Canfield, John Clair, Jr. "Henry Kimbell Hadley: His Life and Works (1871-1937)." Ph.D. diss., Florida State University, 1960.

Hitchcock, Wiley. Crawford, Richard A. *A Celebration of American Music: Words and Music in Honor of H. Wiley Hitchcock.* Ann Arbor, MI: University of Michigan, 1990.

Hodges, Edward. Hodges, Ann. "Edward Hodges: A Survey of His Life and Work." Honors paper, [B.M.] Lawrence University, 1984.

_____. Hodges, Faustina H. *Edward Hodges.* 1896. Reprint, New York: AMS Press, 1970.

_____. Ogasapian, John. *English Cathedral Music in New York: Edward Hodges of Trinity Church.* Richmond, VA: Organ Historical Society, 1994.

Hodges, George. Hodges, Julia Shelley. *George Hodges. A Biography.* New York, London: The Century Co., [c.1926].

Johnson, A. N. Stopp, Jacklin Bolton. "A. N. Johnson, Out of Oblivion." *American Music* 3, no. 2 (Spring 1985): 152-70.

MacDowell, Edward. Levy, Alan. *Edward MacDowell, An American Master.* Lanham, MD: Rowman & Littlefield Publishers, 1998.

_____. Lowens, Margery Morgan. "The New York Years of Edward MacDowell." Ph.D. diss., University of Michigan, 1971.

Oliver, Henry Kemble. Knight, Harold Archie. "The Life and Musical Activities of Henry Kemble Oliver (1800-1885)." Ph.D. diss., University of Iowa, 1988.

Paine, John Knowles, et. al. Bialosky, Marshall. "Some Late Nineteenth Century 'Members' of ASUC: Paine, Parker, MacDowell and Chadwick." Conference Proceedings, American Society of University Composers. Vol. 11-12 (1979): 86-93.

Penn, William Evander. Linder, John Michael. "William Evander Penn: His Contribution to Church Music." DMA diss., Southwestern Baptist Theological Seminary, 1985.

Root, George F. *The Story of a Musical Life: An Autobiography.* 1891. Reprint, New York: AMS Press, 1972.

_____. Carder, Paul H. "George Frederick Root, Pioneer Music Educator: His Contributions to Mass Instruction in Music." Ph.D. diss., University of Maryland, 1971.

Singeberger, John. Gorman, Patrick. "An Analysis of the Choral Music of John Singenberger (1848-1924) as It Relates to the Music Philosophies of the Caecilian Movement." DMA diss., University of Wisconsin, 1994.

Taylor, Raynor. Cuthbert, John. "Raynor Taylor and Anglo-American Musical Life." Ph.D. diss., West Virginia University, 1980.

Titcomb, Everett. Armstrong, Susan. "The Legacy of Everett Titcomb." DMA diss., Boston University, 1990.

Tucker, John Ireland. Knauff, Christopher W. *Doctor Tucker, Priest-Musician: A Sketch Which Concerns the Doings and Thinkings of the Rev. John Ireland Tucker, S.T.D., Including a Brief Converse about the Rise and Progress of Church Music in America.* New York: A. D. F. Randolph Co., 1897.

Walker, William. Eskew, Harry L. "The Life and Work of William Walker." Master's thesis, New Orleans Baptist Theological Seminary, 1960.

Woodbury, Isaac. Copeland, Robert Marshall. "The Life and Works of Isaac Baker Woodbury, 1819-1858." Ph.D. diss., University of Cincinnati, 1974.

Chapter 10

Choral Organizations and Societies

Aliapoulios, Apostolos Anastasios. "A Study of the Adult Amateur Choral Organization in the United States and the Implication for Adult Education." DMA diss., Boston University, 1969.

Apollo Club (Boston). Programs through 1909 (complete set, bound and indexed) and scrapbooks (as well as those of the Orpheus Society). Boston: Boston Public Library.

Arion Society (New York). Constitution of 1890, several Masquerade Ball programs, yearbooks from 1891-1909, leaflets containing *Carneval-Lieder* (1888-1907), a *Mitglieder-Verseichnis* (1912), random yearbooks and personnel lists (1880-1909.) New York: New York Public Library.

Babow, Irving. "The Singing Societies of European Immigrant Groups in San Francisco: 1850-1953." *Journal of the History of the Behavioral Sciences* 5 no. 1 (1969): 10-24.

_____. "The Singing Societies of European Immigrants." *Phylon* 15 (1954): 289-95.

_____. "The Singing Societies of European Immigrants." *Journal of Human Relations* 7 (1959): 504-16.

_____. "Types of Immigrant Singing Societies." *Sociology and Social Research* 39 (1955): 242-47.

Barnes, Mary Musser. "An Historical Survey of the Salt Lake Tabernacle Choir of the Church of Jesus Christ of Latter-Day Saints." Master's thesis, University of Iowa, 1936.

Betterton, William F. *See also chapter 12.*

Blair, Virginia K. "The Singing Societies and Philharmonic Orchestra of Belleville." *Journal of the Illinois State Historical Society* 68 (1975): 386-95.

Bowman, Francis C. *A Review of the Second Triennial Festival of the Handel and Haydn Society, May, 1871*. Boston: Press of Rockwell & Churchill, 1871.

Bradbury, William Frothingham. *History of the Handel and Haydn Society of Boston, Massachusetts. II: From Its 76th through Its 119th Season, 1890-1933*. New York: Da Capo Press, 1979.

Broyles, Michael. "Music and Class Structure in Antebellum Boston." *Journal of the American Musicological Society* 44, no. 3 (1991): 451-93.

Bucker, William Robert. "A History of Chorus America—Association of Professional Vocal Ensembles." DMA diss., University of Missouri, 1991.

Calman, Charles Jeffrey. *The Mormon Tabernacle Choir*. New York: Harper & Row, 1979.

Carroll, Elizabeth Woodruff. "The Bethlehem Bach Festivals." Master's thesis, Union Theological Seminary, 1954.

Cornwall, J. Spencer. *A Century of Singing: The Salt Lake Mormon Tabernacle Choir*. Salt Lake City, UT: The Deseret Book Co., 1958.

Dorndorf, Anton Hubert. "Historical Analysis of the German-American Singing Societies of California with an Evaluation." Master's thesis, University of the Pacific, 1955.

Hass, Oscar. *A Chronological History of the Singers of German Songs in Texas*. New Braunfels, TX: the author, 1948.

Handel and Haydn Society. (Boston, MA) *History of the Handel and Haydn Society*. Boston: A. Mudge & Son, 1889.

_____. *History of the Handel and Haydn Society of Boston, Massachusetts: With a New Table of Contents Prepared by Judith Tick*. 2 vols. New York: Da Capo Press, 1977-79.

_____. Scrapbooks: 1834-1990. Boston: Handel and Haydn Society, 1834-1990.

_____. *Secretary Record Books, 1819-1905*. Boston: Handel and Haydn Society, 1819-1905.

Hall, Roger L. "Old Stoughton Musical Society." *The Sonneck Society Bulletin for American Music* 11, no. 84 (1985).

Hinkle, Leroy Bommer. "The Meaning of Choral Experience to the Adult Membership of the German Singing Societies Comprising the United Singers Federation of Pennsylvania." Ph.D. diss., The Pennsylvania State University, 1987.

History of the Liederkranz of the City of New York, 1847 to 1947, and of the Arion, New York. New York: Dreschel Prints Co., 1948.

Johnson, H. Earle. *Hallelujah, Amen! The Story of the Handel and Haydn Society of Boston.* 1965. Reprint, New York: Da Capo Press, 1981.

Jones, Perry. "The Bethlehem Bach Choir Approaches Its Centennial." *The Choral Journal* 34, no. 9 (April 1994): 13-18.

Kegerreis, Richard. "The Handel Society of Dartmouth." *American Music* 4, no. 2 (Summer 1986): 177-93.

Krehbiel, H. E. *Notes on the Cultivation of Choral Music and the Oratorio Society of New York.* 1884. Reprint, New York: AMS Press, 1970.

Mann, Alfred. "Handel and Haydn: American Choral History." *American Choral Review* 28, no. 4 (October 1986): 3-6.

Mathews, W. S. B. *Lowell Mason and the Higher Art of Music in America. . .* Pt. 1. Chicago: W. S. B. Mathews, 1896.

Metcalf, Henry H. "The Concord Oratorio Society and Its First Annual Festival." *Granite Monthly* 30 (1901): 371-83.

Milligan, Harold V. "An Old Choral Society." *New Music Review* 23 (1924): 191-94.

Nitz, Donald A. "The Norfolk Musical Society, 1814-1820: An Episode in the History of Choral Music in New England." *Journal of Research in Music Education* 16 (1968): 319-28.

Morrow, Mary Sue. "Somewhere between Beer and Wagner: The Cultural and Musical Impact of German Männerchöre in New York and New Orleans." In *Music and Culture in America, 1861-1918,* Michael Saffle, ed. New York and London: Garland Publishing, Inc., 1998: 79-106.

New York Sacred Music Society. *Charter and By-Laws of the New York Sacred Music Society: Instituted 1822, Incorporated 1829.* New York: W. C. Martin, 1842.

Osborne, William. *American Singing Societies and Their Partsongs: Ten Prominent American Composers of the Genre (1860-1940) and the Seminal Singing Societies That Performed the Repertory.* Lawton, OK: American Choral Directors Association, 1994.

Perkins, Charles C., John S. Dwight, and William Frothingham Bradbury. *History of the Handel and Haydn Society of Boston, Massachusetts.* 2 vols. Boston: Alfred Mudge & Son, 1883.

Robinson, Allan. *The Mendelssohn Glee Club: History, Constitution, By-Laws, Officers, Members and Principal Soloists.* New York: G. Schirmer [1930].

Rosewall, Richard Byron. "Singing Schools of Pennsylvania, 1800-1900." Ph.D. diss., University of Minnesota, 1969.

Salzmann, Wilhelm, ed. *Arions Sängerfährt Durch Deutschland und Oesterreich in Wort und Bild.* New York: H. Bartsch, 1893.

Smith, Vernon Leon. The Hampton Institute Choir (Virginia). *See chapter 6.*

Snyder, Suzanne G. "The Indianapolis Männerchor: Contributions to a New Musicality in Midwestern Life." In *Music and Culture in America, 1861-1918.* New York and London: Garland Publishing, Inc., 1998: 111-40.

Sozialistische Liedertafel (NY) and Arbeiter Männerchor (NY). *Musical Archives of Sozialistische Liedertafel (Founded Feb. 1, 1889) and Arbeiter Männerchor (Founded Nov. 1886).* N.p., [1880-1910]. Catalog of the libraries of the two singing societies (photostatic reproduction of manuscript) and remnants of the music, mostly in manuscript.

Walters, Raymond. *The Bethlehem Bach Choir: An Historical Approach and Interpretative Sketch.* 1918. Reprint, New York: AMS Press, 1971.

Winterton, Bonnie Jean Moesser. "A Study of the Choral Program: University of Utah Music Department." Ph.D. diss., University of Utah, 1986.

Chapter 11

Denominational Music

Baldridge, Terry L. "Evolving Tastes in Hymntunes of the Methodist Episcopal Church in the Nineteenth Century." Ph.D. diss., University of Kansas, 1982.

Bender, Harold. S. "The Literature and Hymnology of the Mennonites of Lancaster Country, Pennsylvania." *Mennonite Quarterly Review* 6 (1932): 156-68.

Benton, Franklin Frederick. "Music in the Christian Reformed Church: Its Calvinistic, Systematic Theological Influence and Its Development since 1857." Master's thesis, Mankato State University, 1975.

Bird, Mary Faber. "Early Catholic Church Music in America." Master's thesis, University of Michigan, 1938.

Brennan, Allen John. "Music in the Catholic Church in Philadelphia, 1800-1835." Master's thesis, University of Pennsylvania, 1968.

Cartford, Gerhard M. "Music in the Norwegian Lutheran Church: A Study in the Development in Norway and Its Transfer to America, 1825-1917." Ph.D. diss., University of Minnesota, 1961.

Chorley, E. Clowes. *History of St. Philip's Church in the Highlands, Garrison, New York: Including, up to 1840, St. Peter's Church on the Manor of Cortlandt.* New York: E. S. Gorham, 1912.

_____. *Men and Movements in the American Episcopal Church.* Hamden, CT: Archon Books, 1961.

Christenson, Donald E. "A History of the Early Shakers and Their Music." *Hymn* 39, no. 1 (January 1988): 17-22.

Cook, Harold E. *Shaker Music: A Manifestation of American Folk Culture*. Lewisburg, PA: Bucknell University Press, 1973.

Criswell, Paul Douglas. "The Episcopal Choir School and Choir of Men and Boys in the United States: Its Anglican Tradition, Its American Past and Present." Ph.D. diss., University of Maryland at College Park, 1987.

DeMille, George E. *The Catholic Movement in the American Episcopal Church*. Philadelphia: Church Historical Society, 1941.

_____. *St. Paul's Cathedral, Buffalo, 1817-1967: A Brief History*. [Buffalo? 1967].

Doughty, Gavin Lloyd. "The History and Development of Music in the United Presbyterian Church in the United States of America." Ph.D. diss., University of Iowa, 1966.

Drummond, R. Paul. *A History of Music among Primitive Baptists Since 1800*. Atwood, TN: Christian Baptists Library, 1989.

Farlee, Lloyd Winfield. "A History of the Church Music of the Amana Society, the Community of True Inspiration." Ph.D. diss., University of Iowa, 1966.

Fenton, Kevin A. "Friends University's Singing Quakers: The Development of a Tradition." Ph.D. diss., Florida State University, 1994.

Goodrich, Wallace. "Syllabus of the Course of Lectures upon the Ritual Music of the Protestant Episcopal Church in the United States of America . . . ." Boston: New England Conservatory of Music, 1912.

Graves, Dan. "Singing Out of the Silence: A Survey of Quaker Choral Music." *The Choral Journal* 34, no. 5 (December 1993): 23.

Grider, Rufus. *Historical Notes on Music in Bethlehem, Pennsylvania, from 1741 to 1871*. 1873. Reprint, Winston-Salem: Moravian Music Foundation, 1951.

Grimes, Robert R. *How Shall We Sing in a Foreign Land?" Music of Irish-Catholic Immigrants in the Antebellum United States*. Notre Dame, IN: University of Notre Dame Press, 1996.

Hicks, Michael. *Mormonism and Music: A History*. Urbana, IL: University of Illinois, 1989.

Hall, Roger L. "Shaker Hymnody: An American Communal Tradition." *Hymn* 27, no. 1 (January 1976): 22-29.

Hill, Double E. "A Study of Taste in American Church Music as Reflected in the Music of the Methodist Episcopal Church to 1900." Ph.D. diss., University of Illinois, 1962.

Hohmann, Ruprt Karl. "The Church Music of the Old Order Amish of the United States." Ph.D. diss., Northwestern University, 1959.

Hinks, Donald R. *Brethren Hymn Books and Hymnals, 1720-1884.* Gettysburg, PA: Brethren Heritage Press, 1986.

Jackson, George Pullen. "The Strange Music of the Old Order Amish." *Musical Quarterly* 31, no. 3 (July 1945): 275-88.

Jackson, James Leonard. *Music Practices among Churches of Christ in the United States, 1970.* Master's thesis, University of Oklahoma, 1970.

Jennings, Robert Lee. "A Study of the Historical Development of Choral Ensembles in Selected Lutheran Liberal Arts Colleges in the United States." Ph.D. diss., Michigan State University, 1969.

Jost, Walter James. "The Hymn Tune Tradition of the General Conference Mennonite Church." DMA diss., University of Southern California, 1966.

Kadelbach, Ada. *Die Hymnodie der Mennoniten in Nordamerika (1742-1860): Eine Studie zur Verplanzung. Bewahrung und Umformung europäischer Kirchenliedtradition.* Mainz: the author, 1971.

_____. "Hymns Written by American Mennonites." *Mennonite Quarterly Review* 48 (1974): 343-70.

Kindley, Carolyn E. "Miriam's Timbrel: A Reflection of the Music of Wesleyan Methodism in America, 1843-1899." DA diss., Ball State University, 1985.

Klassen, Roy Leon. "The Influences of Mennonite College Choral Curricula upon Music Practices in American Mennonite Churches." DMA diss., Arizona State University, 1990.

Laycock, H. R. "A History of Music in the Academies of the Latter-Day Saints Church, 1876-1926." Master's thesis, University of Southern California, 1961.

Lehmann, Arnold Otto. "The Music of the Lutheran Church, Synodical Conference, Chiefly the Areas of Missouri, Illinois, Wisconsin, and Neighboring States, 1839-41." Ph.D. diss., Case Western Reserve University, 1967.

McCutchan, Robert Guy. *Our Hymnody: A Manual of the Methodist Hymnal.* New York: Methodist Book Concern, 1937.

Nemmers, Erwin Esser. *Twenty Centuries of Catholic Music.* Milwaukee: Bruce Publishing Co., 1949.

Neve, Paul E. "The Contribution of the Lutheran College Choirs to Music in America." Ph.D. diss., Union Theological Seminary, 1968.

Patterson, Daniel. "Shaker Music." *Communal Societies* 2 (Fall 1982): 53-64.

Patterson, David. *The Shaker Spiritual.* Princeton: Princeton University Press, 1979.

Peasant, Julian S. "The Arts of the African Methodist Episcopal Church as Viewed in the Architecture, Music and Liturgy of the Nineteenth Century." Ph.D. diss., Ohio University, 1992.

Porter, Ellen Jane Lorenz. "The Hymnody of the Evangelical United Brethren Church." *Journal of Theology* 91 (Spring 1987): 74-80.

Purdy, William Earl. "Music in Mormon Culture, 1830-1876." Ph.D. diss., Northwestern University, 1960.

Rasmussen, Jane. "Churchmen Concerned: Music in the Episcopal Church, 1804-1859. A Study of Church Periodicals and Other Ecclesiastical Writings." Ph.D. diss., University of Minnesota, 1983.

Reuss, Francis E. "Catholic Choirs and Choir Music in Philadelphia." *Records of the American Catholic Historical Society of Philadelphia,* 2 (1887): 115-26.

Rice, William Carroll. " A Century of Methodist Music, 1850-1950." Ph.D. diss., University of Iowa, 1953.

Rogal, Samuel. *Guide to the Hymns and Tunes of American Methodism.* Westport, CT: Greenwood Press, 1986.

Rowe, Kenneth E. *Methodist Union Catalog: Pre-1976 Imprints.* Metuchen, NJ: Scarecrow Press, 1975.

Schmitt, Robert J. "A History of Catholic Church Music and Musicians in Milwaukee." Master's thesis, Marquette University, 1968.

Schreiber, William I. "The Hymns of the Amish Ausbund in Philological and Literary Perspective." *Mennonite Quarterly Review* 36, no. 1 (January 1962): 36-60.

Silverberg, Ann Louise. "Cecilian Reform in Baltimore, 1868-1903 (Roman Catholic, American Catholic, Liturgical Music)." Ph.D. diss., University of Illinois at Urbana-Champaign, 1992.

Slaughter, Jay L. "The Role of Music in the Mormon Church, School, and Life." Ph.D. diss., Indiana University, 1964.

Smith, Harold Vaughan. "Oliver C. Hampton and Other Shaker Teacher-Musicians of Ohio and Kentucky." DA diss., Ball State University, 1981.

Springer, Nelson P., and A. J. Klassen. *Mennonite Bibliography, 1631-1961.* Scottsdale, PA: Herald Press, 1977.

Terri, Salli. "The Gift of Shaker Music." *Music Educators Journal* 62, no. 1 (September 1975): 22-35.

Thompson, M. Burnette. "The Significance of the St. Olaf Lutheran Choir in American Choral Music." Master's thesis, Eastman School of Music of the University of Rochester, 1938.

Thompson, Nancy Jane. "A Historical Survey of Music in the Presbyterian Churches in America." Master's thesis, Southern Baptist Theological Seminary, 1948.

Washington, Louis Cope. *Historical Sketch of the Episcopal Church in the City of Rochester, New York.* [Rochester, NY]: printed for the Rochester Clericus, 1908.

West, Edward N. "History and development of Music in the American [Episcopal] Church." *Historical Magazine of the Protestant Episcopal Church* 14 (1945): 15-37.

_____. "The Music of Old Trinity." *Historical Magazine of the Protestant Episcopal Church* 16 (1947): 100-24.

Wilson, Ruth Mack. "Episcopal Music in America: The British Legacy." *Musical Times* 124 (July 1983): 447-50.

Wohlgemuth, Paul William. "Mennonite Hymnals Published in the English Language." DMA diss., University of Southern California, 1956.

Wolf, Edward Christopher. "Lutheran Church Music in America during the Eighteenth and Early Nineteenth Centuries." Ph.D. diss., University of Illinois at Urbana-Champaign, 1960.

_____. "Lutheran Hymnody and Music Published in America, 1700-1850: A Descriptive Bibliography." *Concordia Historical Institute Quarterly* 50 (1977): 164-85.

Yoder, Paul Marvin. "Nineteenth-Century Sacred Music of the Mennonite Church in the United States." Ph.D. diss., Florida State University, 1961.

Zen, Allen. "A Study of the Boy Choir in the Protestant Episcopal Church." Master's thesis, University of Southern California, 1963.

Chapter 12

Regional Studies

Abbott, Jacob. "The Village Choir." In *New England and Her Institutions: By One of Her Sons.* London: R. B. Seeley and W. Burnside, 1835: 303-93.

Allwardt, Anton Paul. "Sacred Music in New York City: 1800-1850." Ph.D. diss., Union Theological Seminary, 1950.

Anderson, Fletcher Clark. "A History of Choral Music in Birmingham, Alabama." Ph.D. diss, University of Georgia, 1978.

Andrus, Helen J. *A Century of Music in Poughkeepsie, 1802-1911.* Poughkeepsie, NY: Frank B. Howard, 1912.

Atherton, Lewis. *Main Street on the Middle Border.* Bloomington: Indiana University Press, 1954.

"The Atlanta Sängerfest." *Musical Courier* (24 May 1911): 9.

Baader, Mary Lenore. "The Music of Early Wisconsin." Master's thesis, Catholic University of America, 1967.

Betterton, William F. "Early Choral Groups: Music in Early Davenport." *The Palimpsest* 45, no. 7 (July 1964): 283-292.

_____. "Music in Early Davenport." *The Palimpsest* 45, no. 6 (June 1964): 273-304.

_____. "The Saengerfest of 1898: Music in Early Davenport." *The Palimpsest* 45, no. 7 (July 1964): 293-300.

Baltzell, Winston J. "Music in American Cities. The Three Lake Cities: Buffalo, Cleveland and Detroit." *Musician* 18, no. 6 (1913): 369-73.

Baynham, Edward Gladstone. *A History of Pittsburgh Music, 1758-1958.* Pittsburgh, PA: n.p., 1970.

Bellinger, Martha F. "Music in Indianapolis, 1821-1900." *Indiana Magazine of History* (December 1945): 345-62.

Betterton, William F. "A History of Music in Davenport, Iowa, before 1900." Ph.D. diss., University of Iowa, 1962.

Bittner, Robert E. "The Concert Life and the Musical Stage in New Orleans Up to the Construction of the French Opera House." Master's thesis, Louisiana State University, 1953.

Bohlman, Philip Vilas. "Music in the Culture of German-Americans in North-Central Wisconsin." Ph.D. diss., University of Illinois at Urbana-Champaign, 1980.

Boudreaux, Peggy Cecile. "Music Publishing in New Orleans in the Nineteenth Century." Master's thesis, Louisiana State University, 1977.

Breitmayer, Douglas Reece. "Seventy-Five Years of Sacred Music in Cleveland, Ohio, 1800-1875." Master's thesis, Union Theological Seminary, 1951.

Brown, Lilla Jean. "Music in the History of Dallas, Texas, 1841-1900." Master's thesis, University of Texas at Austin, 1947.

Carden, Joy C. *Music in Lexington before 1840*. Lexington: Lexington-Fayette County Historic Commission, 1980.

Carroll, Lucy Ellen. "Three Centuries of Song: Pennsylvania's Choral Composers, 1681 to 1981." DMA diss., Combs College of Music, 1982.

Cawthon, John A. "Make a Joyful Noise: Selected North Louisiana Musicians." *North Louisiana Historical Association Journal* 9, no. 1 (1978): 29-35.

Choir Record of a New England Church, 1845-1862: A Book Kept by Nathaniel Head, in Charge of the Choir in Rev. Job Robert's Church, Fairhaven, Mass. from 1845-62. Held by Boston Public Library.

Coker, John W. "Charleston, South Carolina, a Century of Music, 1732-1833." Ph.D. diss., University of Cincinnati, 1955.

Cole, Ronald Fred. "Music in Portland, Maine, from Colonial Times through the 19th Century." Ph.D. diss., Indiana University, 1975.

Crews, Emma Katherine. "A History of Music in Knoxville, Tennessee, 1791 to 1910." Ed.D. diss., Florida State University, 1961.

Dart, Harold. "An Introduction to Selected New England Composers of the Late Nineteenth Century." *Music Educators Journal* 60, no. 3 (November 1973): 47-53, 89-92. Includes discussion of Horatio Parker's *Hora Novissima*.

Denniston, Robert James. "The Development of Sacred Music at Chautauqua." Master's thesis, Union Theological Seminary, 1956.

DiBiase, Mildred. "A Survey of Music Composed and Published in Buffalo Prior to 1900." Master's thesis, Canisius College, 1952.

Dinneen, William and Joyce Ellen Mangler. [Early Music in Rhode Island Churches.] Four articles that appeared in successive issues of *Rhode Island History* for 1958.

Doran, Carol Ann. "The Influence of Raynor Taylor and Benjamin Carr on Church Music in Philadelphia at the Beginning of the Nineteenth Century." 2 vols. Ph.D. diss., University of Rochester, 1970.

Duggan, Mary Kay. "Music Publishing and Printing in San Francisco before the Earthquake and Fire of 1906." *Kemble Occasional* 34 (Fall 1980).

Eaton, Quaintance, ed. *Musical U.S.A.* New York: Allen, Towne & Heath, 1949.

Earle, A. M. "Old-Time Church Music in New England." *Outlook* 48 (12 November 1893): 933-34.

Edwards, George Thornton. *Music and Musicians of Maine, by George Thornton Edwards; Being a History of the Progress of Music in the Territory Which Has Come to be known as the State of Maine, from 1604 to 1928.* Portland, ME: The Southworth Press, 1928.

Engel, Kathleyn. "Musical Life in Boston and New York, 1849-1854." Master's thesis, University of Michigan, 1947.

Engelson, Robert Allen. "A History of Adult Community Choirs in Charlotte, North Carolina: 1865-1918." DMA diss., Arizona State University, 1994.

Falsone, Patricia Jane. "Secular Music in Worcester, Massachusetts from the Turn of the 18th Century to the Onset of the Civil War (1800-1863)." Master's thesis, University of Lowell, 1980.

Ferguson, James Smith. "A History of Music in Vicksburg, Mississippi, 1820-1900." Ed.D. diss., University of Michigan, 1970.

Fisher, Robert. *See chapter 8.*

Ffrench Florence, comp. *Music and Musicians in Chicago: The City's Leading Artists, Organizations and Art Buildings: Progress and Development. . . .* Chicago: the author, 1899.

Freedman, Frederick. "Music in Ohio: A Preliminary Bibliography." [Cleveland, 1974.]

Fuller, Marion Kendall. "Vienna and Hartford in 1850: Being a Musical, Social and Educational Picture of the Two Cities at Mid-Century." M.Mus.Ed., University of Hartford, 1958.

Gerson, Robert A. *Music in Philadelphia.* 1940. Reprint, Westport, CT: Greenwood Press, 1970.

Gillis, Frank James. "Minnesota Music in the Nineteenth Century: A Guide to Sources and Resources." Master's thesis, University of Minnesota, 1958.

Gertjejansen, Kenneth. "Music in Minnesota's History." Master's thesis, Minnesota State Teachers College at Mankato, 1956.

Grossman, F. Karl. *A History of Music in Cleveland.* Cleveland, OH: Case Western Reserve University, 1972.

Hammond, Paul Garnett. "Music in Urban Revivalism in the Northern United States, 1800-1835." DMA diss., Southern Baptist Theological Seminary, 1974.

Haskins, John C. "Music in the District of Columbia." Master's thesis, Catholic University of America, 1952.

Hehr, Milton G. "Musical Activities in Salem, Massachusetts: 1783-1823." Ph.D. diss., Boston University, 1963.

Hindman, John Joseph. "Concert Life in Ante Bellum Charleston." Ph.D. diss., University of North Carolina at Chapel Hill, 1971.

Hirtzel, Robert Louis. "A History of Music in Fort Vancouver and the City of Vancouver, Washington, 1824 to 1950." Master's thesis, Portland University, 1953.

History of Music in San Francisco. 7 vols. Works Projects Administration. California. San Francisco, 1939-1942. Reprint, New York: AMS Press, 1972.

Johnson, Francis Hall. *Musical Memories of Hartford: Drawn from Records Public and Private.* 1931. Reprint, New York: AMS Press, 1970.

Johnson, Harold Earle. *Musical Interludes in Boston, 1795-1830.* 1903. Reprint, New York: AMS Press, 1967.

Keefer, Lubov. *Baltimore's Music: The Haven of the American Composer.* Baltimore: J. H. Furst, 1962.

Kennedy, Robert Allen. "A History and Survey of Community Music in Mobile, Alabama." Ph.D. diss., Florida State University, 1960.

Kinney, Mary Gene. "Public Concert Life in Boston, 1852-1857, as Seen through *Dwight's Journal of Music.* Master's thesis, University of Southern California, 1972.

Klein, Hermann. *Unmusical New York: A Brief Criticism of Triumphs, Failures, and Abuses.* London and New York: John Lane, 1910.

Kleinsasser, Jerome Stewart. "Nineteenth-Century Twin City Choral Activities." Ph.D. diss., University of Minnesota, 1972.

Kmen, Henry A. *Music in New Orleans: The Formative Years, 1791-1841.* Baton Rouge: Louisiana State University Press, 1966.

Knight, Ellen. "Music in Winchester, Massachusetts: A Community Portrait, 1830-1925." *American Music* 11, no. 3 (Fall 1993): 263-82.

Kozlowski, Marianne Clare. "Music in Chicago, 1830 to 1850." Master's thesis, University of Illinois at Urbana-Champaign, 1977.

Krehbiel, Henry E. "Church Music in New York: Some Phases in Its Development." *Church Music Review* 3 (1903-4): 329-31.

_____. *Review of the New York Musical Season, 1885-1890.* 5 vols. New York: Novello, Ewer & Co., 1886-90.

Krohn, Ernst C. *Missouri Music.* 1924. Reprint, New York: Da Capo Press, 1971.

Lahee, Henry C. "A Century of Choral Singing in New England." *New England Magazine* 26 (1902): 102-17.

Larson, Esther. "The History of Music in Los Angeles." Master's thesis, University of Southern California, 1930.

Lebar, Elaine E. Lebowitz. "History of Musical Development in Missouri." Master's thesis, University of Missouri at Columbia, 1950.

Leaver, Robin A. "New Light on the Prehistory of the Bach Choir of Bethlehem." *Bach* 22, no. 2 (Fall-Winter 1991): 24-34.

Lincoln,. Jean. "Music in Michigan before 1860." Master's thesis, Michigan State University, 1939.

Linscome, Sanford Abel. "A History of Musical Development in Denver, Colorado, 1858-1908." DMA diss., University of Texas at Austin, 1970.

McDaniel, Stanley Robert. "Church Song and the Cultivated Tradition in New England and New York." DMA diss., University of Southern California, 1983.

McKinley, Ann. "Music for the Dedication Ceremonies of the World's Columbian Exposition in Chicago, 1892." *American Music* 3, no. 1 (Spring 1985): 42-51.

Mangler, Joyce Ellen. *Rhode Island Music and Musicians, 1733-1850.* Detroit, MI: Information Service, 1965. (Detroit Studies in Music Bibliography, No. 7.)

Marco, Guy A., Ann Garfield, and Sharon Paugh Ferris. *Information on Music: A Handbook of Reference Sources in European Languages, Volume II, The Americas.* Littleton, CO: Libraries Unlimited, 1977.

Metcalf, Frank J. "History of Sacred Music in the District of Columbia." *Records of the Columbia Historical Society* 28 (1926): 175-202.

Myracle, Kay Ferree. "Music in Memphis, 1880-1900." Master's thesis, Memphis State University, 1975.

Nitz, Donald Arthur. "The Norfolk Musical Society, 1814-1820." *Journal of Research in Music Education* 4 (1968): 319-28.

Norris, Ethel Maureen. *See chapter 6.*

Olsen, Audrey L. *St. Louis Germans, 1850-1920: The Nature of an Immigrant Community and Its Relation to the Assimilation Process.* New York: Arno Press, 1980.

Orr, N. Lee. *Alfredo Barili and the Rise of Classical Music in Atlanta.* Atlanta, GA: Scholars Press, 1996.

Osburn, Mary Hubbel. *Ohio Composers and Musical Authors.* Columbus, OH: F. J. Heer Printing Co., 1942.

Packer, Mina Belle. "A Brief Survey of Sacred Music in Pittsburgh, Pennsylvania, Past and Present." Master's thesis, Union Theological Seminary, 1955.

Paige, Paul Eric. "Chamber Music in Boston: The Harvard Musical Association." *Journal of Research in Music Education* 28, no. 2 (Summer 1970): 134-42.

_____. "Musical Organizations in Boston: 1830-1850." Ph.D. diss., Boston University, 1967.

Pierce, Frank H., III. *The Washington Sängerbund: A History of German Song and German Culture in the Nation's Capital.* Washington, DC: The Washington Sängerbund, 1981.

Pohly, Linda L. "Music in Wichita, 1870-1906." Master's thesis, Wichita State University, 1978.

_____."The Kansas Musical Jubilee, 1893-1903: Prelude to School Music Contests." *Bulletin of Historical Research in Music Education* 16, no. 1 (September 1994): 17-28.

Price, Robert Bates. "A History of Music in Northern Louisiana until 1900." DMA diss., Catholic University of America, 1977.

Rauchle, Bob Cyrus. "The Social and Cultural Contributions of the German Population in Memphis, Tennessee, 1848-1880." Master's thesis, University of Tennessee, 1964.

Reagan, Ann Bakamjian. "Art Music in Milwaukee in the Late Nineteenth Century, 1850-1900." Ph.D. diss., University of Wisconsin at Madison, 1980.

Redway, Virginia Larkin. *Music Directory of Early New York City. . .* New York: The New York Public Library, 1941.

Reinsasser, Jerome Stewart. "Nineteenth-Century Twin-City Choral Activities." Ph.D. diss., University of Minnesota, 1972.

Robertson, Reba. "Musical History of Cincinnati." Master's thesis, Cincinnati Conservatory of Music, 1941.

Robertson, Susanne M. Scott. "Musical Activity in Lowell, Massachusetts, from 1825 to 1900." Master's thesis, Indiana University, 1973.

Rogers, Delmer Dalzell. "Nineteenth-Century Music in New York City as Reflected in the Career of George Frederick Bristow." Ph.D. diss., University of Michigan, 1967.

Rohrer, Getrude Martin. *Music and Musicians of Pennsylvania.* Compiled under the Auspices of the Pennsylvania Federation of Music Clubs. 1940. Reprint, Port Washington: Kennikat Press, 1970.

Salisgian, Robert K. "Music in Worcester, Massachusetts, from Colonial Times through the Nineteenth Century." Ph.D. diss., Michigan State University, 1964.

Seidensticker, Oswald. *See chapter 24.*

Seip, Oswell J. "Pennsylvania German Choral Books." *Proceedings of the Lehigh County Historical Society* (1944): 39-43.

Seymour, Margaret R. "Music in Lincoln, Nebraska, in the Nineteenth Century: A Study of the Musical Culture of a Frontier Society." Master's thesis, University of Nebraska, 1968.

Shifflet, Anne Louise. "Church Music and Musical Life in Frederick, Maryland, 1745-1845." Master's thesis, American University, 1971.

Simons, Elizabeth Potter. *Music in Charleston from 1732 to 1919.* Charleston, SC: J. J. Furlong & Son, Inc., 1927.

Spell, Lota M. *Music in Texas: A Survey of One Aspect of Cultural Progress.* Austin, TX: privately printed, 1936.

Staater, H. Ray. "The First Quarter Century of Music in Chicago (1835-1860)." Master's thesis, DePaul University, 1940.

Standish, L. W. *The Old Stoughton Musical Society: An Historical and Informative Record of the Oldest Choral Society in America. . . .* Stoughton, MA: Stoughton Printing Co., 1929.

Steinhaus, Walter E. "Music in the Cultural Life of Macon, Georgia– 1823-1900." Ph.D., diss., Florida State University, 1973.

Stoutamire, Albert L. "A History of Music in Richmond, Virginia, from 1742-1865." Ph.D. diss., Florida State University, 1960.

_____. *Music of the Old South: Colony to Confederacy.* Rutherford: Fairleigh Dickinson University Press, 1972.

Summey, Patricia Ann. "A History of Musical Activities in Greenville, South Carolina, 1800-1900." M.Mus. Ed., Florida State University, 1960.

Swan, Howard. *Music in the Southwest, 1825-1950.* 1952. Reprint, New York: Da Capo Press, 1977.

Swan, John C. *Music in Boston: Readings from the First Three Centuries.* Boston: Trustees of the Public Library of the City of Boston, 1977.

Teal, Mary Evelyn Durden. "Musical Activities in Detroit from 1701- 1870." Ph.D. diss., University of Michigan, 1964.

Thompson, James William. "Music and Musical Activities in New England, 1800-1838." Ph.D. diss., Vanderbilt University, 1962.

Thompson, Reed Paul. "Eighty Years in Music in St. George, Utah, 1861-1941." Master's thesis, Brigham Young University, 1952.

Thorson, Theodore W. "A History of Music Publishing in Chicago, 1850-1960." Ph.D. diss., Northwestern University, 1961.

Thrasher, Herbert Chandler, and Dorothy Joslin Pearce. *250 Years of Music in Providence, Rhode Island, 1636-1886.* [Providence, RI]: Rhode Island Federation of Music Clubs, 1942.

Tvrdy, Helen. "A Century of Music in Omaha, 1854-1954." Master's thesis, Creighton University, 1954.

Upton, George P. *Musical Memories: My Recollection of Celebrities of the Half Century 1850-1900.* Chicago: A. C. McClurg & Co., 1908.

Weston, Geoffrey C. "Music and Musicians in Central Connecticut to About 1825." Ph.D., diss., New York University, 1968.

Wetzel, Richard D. *Frontier Musicians on the Connoquenessing, Wabash, and Ohio: A History of the Music and Musicians of George Rapp's Harmony Society (1805-1906).* Athens, OH: Ohio University Press, 1976.

_____. "The Music of George Rapp's Harmony Society: 1805-1906." Ph.D. diss., University of Pittsburgh, 1970.

Williams, G. W. "Charleston Church Music, 1562-1833." *Journal of the American Musicological Society* 7 (Spring 1954): 35-40.

Williams, Grier Moffat. "A History of Music in Jacksonville, Florida, from 1822-1922." Ph.D. diss., Florida State University, 1961.

Wilson, George H. *The Boston Musical Year Book.* Vol. I: Season of 1883-84; Vol. II: Season of 1884-85. Boston: Geo. H. Ellis Printer, 1884-85.

_____. *The Boston Musical Year Book and Musical Year in the United States.* Vol. III: Season of 1885-86. Boston: Geo. H. Ellis Printers, 1886.

_____. *The Musical Year-Book of the United States. A Record of Musical Performance in the Country with the Boston Season in Detail.* Vol. IV: Season of 1886-87. Boston: G. H. Wilson, 1887.

Wilson, James Grant, ed. *The Memorial History of the City of New York: From Its First Settlement to the Year 1892.* Vol. 4. New York: New York History Co., 1893.

Winsor, Justin, ed. *The Memorial History of Boston, Including Suffolk County, Massachusetts, 1630-1880.* Vol. IV. The Last Hundred Years. Boston: Osgood, 1881.

Wolfe, A. D. "Nineteenth-Century New Orleans Composers." Master's thesis, North Texas State University, 1968.

Wolz, Larry R. "A Survey of Concert Life in Texas during the Nineteenth Century." Master's thesis, Texas Christian University, 1976.

Wyrick, Charles R. "Concert and Criticism in Cincinnati, 1840-1850." Master's thesis, University of Cincinnati, 1965.

Chapter 13

Hymns and Gospel Songs

Albertson, Wayne Frederick. "Narcissism and Destiny: A Study of the Life and Work of Fanny J. Crosby." Ph.D. diss., Princeton Theological Seminary, 1992.

Andrews, Edward E. *The Gift to be Simple. Songs, Dances and Rituals of the American Shakers.* 1940. Reprint, New York: Dover Publications, 1962.

Barber, Samuel. "The Choral Style of the Wings Over Jordan Choir." DMA diss., University of Cincinnati, 1979.

Baxter, Mrs. J. R. ("Ma"), and Videt Polk. *Gospel Song Writer's Biography.* Dallas: Stamps-Baxter, [1971].

Benson, Louis F. *The English Hymn: Its Development and Use in Worship.* London: Hodder and Stoughton, 1915.

Blackwell, L. S. *The Wings of the Dove: The Story of Gospel Music in America.* Norfolk, VA: Donning, 1978.

Brobston, Stanley Heard. "A Brief History of White Southern Gospel Music and a Study of Selected Amateur Family Gospel Music Singing Groups in Rural Georgia." Ph.D. diss., New York University, 1977.

Burt, Jesse, and Duane Allen. *The History of Gospel Music.* Nashville: K & S Press, 1971.

Butterworth, Hezekiah. *The Story of the Hymns; Or, Hymns That Have a History.* New York: American Tract Society, 1875.

_____. *The Story of the Tunes: For Home Reading, Praise Meeting, and Lectures on Sacred Music.* New York: American Tract Society, 1890.

Brown, Theron, and Hezekiah Butterworth. *The Story of the Hymns and Tunes.* 1906. 1923. Reprint, Grosse Point, MI: Scholarly Press, 1968.

Card, Edith Bryson. "Development of the American Hymn Tune, 1800-1850." Master's thesis, Florida State University, 1975.

Christ-Janer, Albert, Charles W. Hughes, and Carleton Sprague Smith. *American Hymns Old and New.* New York: Columbia University Press, 1980.

Christenson, Donald E. "A History of the Early Shakers and Their Music." *The Hymn* 39, no. 1 (1988): 17-22.

Clark, Keith C. *A Selective Bibliography for the Study of Hymns, 1980.* 2nd ed. Papers of the Hymn Society 33. Springfield, OH: Hymn Society of America, 1980.

Creamer, David. *Methodist Hymnody, with Critical and Historical Observations.* New York: Joseph Longking, 1848.

Cross, Virginia Ann. "The Development of Sunday School Hymnody in the United States of America, 1816-1869." DMA diss., New Orleans Baptist Theological Seminary, 1985.

DeRemer, Bernard D. "When Sankey Sang." *Church Musician* 17, no. 11 (1966): 6-9.

Detrick, Daniel A. "The Hymn Society of America's Collection of Hymnals and Hymnological Materials: An Annotated Index." Master's thesis, Texas Christian University, 1988.

Diehl, Katharine S. *Hymns and Tunes. An Index.* New York: Scarecrow Press, 1966.

Downey, James Cecil. "The Gospel Hymn 1875-1930." Master's thesis, University of Southern Mississippi, 1963.

_____. "The Music of American Revivalism." Ph.D. diss., Tulane University, 1968.

Drummond, Robert Paul. "A History of Music among Primitive Baptists since 1800." Ph.D. diss., University of Northern Colorado, 1986.

Ellinwood, Leonard Webster, and Elizabeth Lockwood. *Bibliography of American Hymnals: Compiled by the Hymn Society of America from the Files of the Dictionary of American Hymnology.* New York: University Music Editions, 1983. 27 microfiche.

_____, ed. *Dictionary of American Hymnology: First Line Index.* New York: University Music Editions, 1984. 179 microfilm reels.

_____. *Sisters of Sacred Song: A Catalog of British and American Women Hymnodists. A Selected Listing of Women Hymnodists in Great Britain and America*. New York: Garland, 1981.

Escott, Harry. *Isaac Watts, Hymnographer: A Study of Beginnings, Development and Philosophy of the English Hymn*. London: Independent Press, Lt., 1962.

Eskew, Harry L. *Index of the Hymn, 1949-1972*. Springfield, OH: the Hymn Society of America,

_____. "William Walker, 1809-1875: Popular Southern Hymnist." *The Hymn* 15, no. 5 (1964): 5-13.

Eskew, Harry L. and Hugh T. McElrath. *Sing with Understanding*. Nashville, TN: Church Street Press, 1995.

Flew, R. Newton. *The Hymns of Charles Wesley: A Study of Their Structure*. London: Epworth Press, 1953.

Foote, Arthur I. *Henry Wilder Foote, Hymnologist*. New York: Hymn Society of America, 1968.

Foote, Henry Wilder. *Three Centuries of American Hymnody*. 1940. Reprint, with a new appendix. Hamden, CT: Archon Books, 1968.

Goodenough, Caroline Leonard. *High Lights on Hymnals and Their Hymns*. 1931. Reprint, New York: AMS Press, 1974.

Gould, Nathaniel Duren. *Music Prosody; Containing a Selection of Hymns, with Concise Directions for the Appropriate Application of Music to Words: Designed for the Use and Improvement of Individuals and Singing Choirs*. Boston: Richardson, Lord & Holbrook, 1830.

Graham, Fred Kimball. "'With One Heart and One Voice': A Core Repertory of Hymn Tunes Published for Use in the Methodist Episcopal Church in the United States, 1808-1878." Ph.D. diss., Drew University, 1991.

Hall, J. H. *Biography of Gospel Song and Hymn Writers*. 1914. Reprint, New York: AMS Press, 1971.

Hall, James W. "The Tune-Book in American Culture, 1800-1820." Ph.D. diss., University of Pennsylvania, 1967.

Hawn, C. Michael. "The Tie That Binds: A List of Ecumenical Hymns in English Language Hymnals Published in Canada and the United States since 1976." *The Hymn* 48, no. 3 (July 1997): 25-37.

Higginson, J. V. "Hymnody in the American Indian Missions." *The Catholic Choirmaster* 40 (Winter 1954): 161-76.

Hitchcock, H. W. "An Important American Tune-Book." *Journal of the American Musicological Society* 8 (Fall 1955): 225-26.

Horn, Dorothy D. "A Study of the Folk Hymns of Southeastern America." Ph.D. diss., University of Rochester, 1953.

Howell, Lillian Pope. "Lowell Mason, Composer of Hymn-Tunes." Master's thesis, Southern Baptist Theological Seminary, 1948.

Hughes, Charles W. *American Hymns Old and New: Notes on the Hymns and Biographies of the Authors and Composers.* New York: Columbia University Press, 1980.

Jackson, George Pullen. *Index to the George Pullen Jackson Collection of Southern Hymnody, 1800-1953.* Los Angeles: University Library, University of California, CA: 1964.

Jensen, David G. comp. *An American Folk-Hymn Index of Seven Shape-Note Hymnals.* Portland, OR: the author, n.d.

Kahel, Lois. "A Survey of American Hymnody during the First Half of the Nineteenth Century." Master's thesis, Union Theological Seminary, 1946.

Kidder, D. H. "John Greenleaf Whittier's Contribution to Hymnody." *Hymn* 8 (October 1957): 105-10.

Krouse, Elizabeth Alma. "The Treatment of Death in Selected Nineteenth Century Hymnals and Tunebooks from 1835 to 1870." DMA diss., University of Missouri at Kansas City, 1990.

Kroeger, Karl. *American Fuguing Tunes, 1770-1829: A Descriptive Catalog.* Westport, CT: Greenwood Press, 1994.

Lawson, John. *The Wesley Hymns.* Grand Rapids, MI: Francis Asbury Press, 1987.

Livingston, John Henry, and The Reformed Church in America. *The Psalms and Hymns of the Reformed Dutch Church in North America.* New Brunswick, NJ: Rutgers Press, 1826.

Lorenz, Ellen Jane. *The Devil's Good Tunes: The Secular in Protestant Hymnody.* Dayton, OH: E. J. Porter, 1978.

_____. *Hymnbook Collections of North America.* Fort Worth, TX: Hymn Society of America, 1987.

_____. *Nineteenth-Century American Songs and Hymns as a Reflection of the Romantic Movement.* Dayton, OH: E. J. Porter, 1978.

Lovelace, Austin C. *The Anatomy of Hymnody.* New York: Abingdon Press, [1965].

McCommon, Paul C. "The Influence of Charles Wesley's Hymns on Baptist Theology." Ph.D. diss., Southern Baptist Theological Seminary, 1948.

McCutchan, Robert Guy. *Hymn Tune Names: Their Sources and Significance.* 1957. Reprint, St. Clair Shores: Scholarly Press, 1974.

McDormand, Thomas B., and Frederic S. Corssman. *Judson Concordance to Hymnns.* Valley Forge, PA: Judson Press, 1965.

McKeller, Hugh D. "A History of the Hymn Society in the United States and Canada, 1922-1997." *Hymn* 48, no. 3 (July 1997): 8-16.

Manning, B. L. *The Hymns of Wesley and Watts.* London: Epworth Press, 1942.

Marini, Stephen A. "Hymnody in the Religious Communal Societies of Early America." *Communal Societies* 2 (Fall 1982): 1-25.

Martin, Raymond Jones. "The Transition from Psalmody to Hymnody in Southern Presbyterianism, 1753-1901." SMD diss., Union Theological Seminary, 1963.

Mauney, Richard Steadman. "The Development of Missionary Hymnody in the United States of America in the Nineteenth Century." DMA diss., Southwestern Baptist Theological Seminary, 1993.

Messenger, Ruth Ellis, and Helen E. Pfatteicher. *A Short Bibliography for the Study of Hymns.* New York: Hymn Society of America, 1964.

Morgan, Catharine. "Sacred Folk Song in America." *American Guild of Organists Quarterly* 12 (1967): 54-60.

Murrell, Irvin Henry, Jr. "An Examination of Southern Ante-bellum Baptist Hymnals and Tunebooks as Indicators of the Congregational Hymn and Tune Repertoires of the Period with an Analysis of Representative Tunes." DMA diss., New Orleans Baptist Theological Seminary, 1984.

Music, David W. *Hymnology. A Collection of Source Readings.* Lanham, MD: Scarecrow Press, 1996: 189-210.

New England Pastor. *Practical Hints on Church Music and Congregational Singing. . . . With an Appendix about Hymn Books and Hymn and Tune Books.* New Haven, CT: Peck, White & Peck, 1859.

Ninde, Edward S. *The Story of the American Hymn.* 1926. Reprint, New York: AMS Press, 1975.

Parks, Edna. *The Hymns and Hymn Tunes Found in the English Metrical Psalters*. New York: Coleman-Ross Co., 1966.

_____. *Early English Hymns: An Index*. Metuchen, NJ: Scarecrow Press, 1972.

Patterson, Daniel W. "Hunting for the American White Spiritual: A Survey of Scholarship, with Discography." *ARSC Journal* 3, no. 1 [1971]: 7-18.

_____. "The Influence of Inspiration and Discipline upon the Development of the Shaker Spiritual." *Shaker Quarterly* 6 (1966): 77-87.

_____. *The Shaker Spiritual*. Princeton, NJ: Princeton University Press, 1979.

Perrin, Phil D. "Theoretical Introductions in American Tunebooks from 1800-1860." DMA diss., Southwestern Baptist Theological Seminary, 1968.

Phelps, Austin, E. A. Park, and D. L. Furber. *Hymns and Choirs: Or, the Matter and the Manner of the Service of Song in the House of the Lord*. Andover, MA: W. F. Draper, 1860.

Porter, Ellen Jane Lorenz. "A Treasure of Camp-Meeting Spirituals." Ph.D. diss., Union Graduate School, Ohio, 1978.

_____. "William B. Bradbury, the Campmeeting Spiritual and the Gospel Song." *Hymn* 34, no. 1 (1983): 34-40.

Porter, Thomas H. "Dissertations and Theses Related to American Hymnody, 1964-1978." *Hymn* 30 (1979): 199-204, 221; vol. 31 (1980): 48-53; vol. 32 (1981): 35-36; vol. 33 (1982): 41-43; vol. 34 (1983): 40-41; vol. 35 (1984): 102-104.

Ralston, Jack L. "A Bibliography of Currently Available Early American Tunebook Reprints." *Hymn* 33 (1982): 212-15.

Revitt, Paul J., comp. *The George Pullen Jackson Collection of Southern Hymnody: A Bibliography*. Los Angeles: UCLA Library Occasional Papers, Number 13, 1964.

Reynolds, William J. *Songs of Glory: Stories of 300 Great Hymns and Gospel Songs*. Grand Rapids, MI: Zondervan Books, 1990.

_____. *A Survey of Christian Hymnody*. New York: Holt, Rinehart and Winston, 1963.

Rogal, Samuel. *See chapter 11*.

Ronander, A. C. "The Hymnody of Congregationalism." *Hymn* 8 (January 1957): 5-14.

Rothenbusch, Esther Heidi. "The Role of 'Gospel Hymns Nos. 1 to 6,' 1875-1894, in American Revivalism." Ph.D. diss., University of Michigan, 1991.

Routley, Eric. *Church Music and Theology.* Philadelphia: Muhlenberg Press, 1959.

_____. *The Musical Wesleys.* New York: Oxford University Press, 1968.

Sankey, Ira D. *Sankey's Story of the Gospel Hymns, and of Sacred Songs and Solos.* Philadelphia: Sunday School Times, 1906.

_____. *My Life and Sacred Song.* London: Hodder and Stoughton, 1906.

Sims, John Norman. "The Hymnody of the Camp-Meeting Tradition." SMD diss., Union Theological Seminary, 1960.

Sizer, Sandra Sue. "Revival Waves and Home Fires: The Rhetoric of Late Nineteenth-Century Gospel Hymns." Ph.D. diss., University of Chicago, 1976.

_____. *Gospel Hymns and Social Religion: The Rhetoric of Nineteenth-Century Revivalism.* Philadelphia: Temple University Press, 1978.

Smith, Timothy Alan. "The Southern Folk-Hymn, 1800-1860: Notes on Performance Practice." *Choral Journal* 23, no. 7 (March 1983): 23-29.

Smucker, David Joseph. "Philip Paul Bliss and the Musical, Cultural and Religious Sources of the Gospel Music Tradition in the United States, 1850-1876." Ph.D. diss., Boston University, 1981.

Stanley, D. H. "The Gospel-Singing Convention in South Georgia." *Journal of American Folklore* 95, no. 375 (1982): 1-32.

Steel, David Warren. "John Wyeth and the Development of Southern Folk Hymnody." In *Music from the Middle Ages through the Twentieth Century: Essays in Honor of Gywnn McPeek.* New York: Gordon and Breach Science Publishers, 1988.

Stebbins, George C. *Reminiscences and Gospel Hymn Stories.* 1924. Reprint, New York: AMS Press, 1971.

Stevenson, Arthur L. *The Story of Southern Hymnology.* 1931. Reprint, New York: AMS Press, 1975.

Studwell, William E. *Christmas Carols: A Reference Guide.* New York: Garland, 1985.

Sydnor, James Rawlings, ed. *A Short Bibliography for the Study of Hymns*. The Papers of the Hymn Society. Springfield, OH: The Hymn Society of America, Inc., 1964.

Tamke, Susan S. *Make a Joyful Noise unto the Lord: Hymns as a Reflection of Victorian Social Attitudes*. [Athens, OH]: Ohio University Press, 1978.

Tanner, Donald. "An Analysis of Assemblies of God Hymnology." Ph.d. diss., University of Minnesota, 1974.

Temperley, Nicholas. *The Hymn Tune Index: A Census of English-Language Hymn Tunes in Printed Sources from 1535 to 1820*. 4 vols. New York: Oxford University Press, 1998.

Thiessen, Don. *Psalms, Hymns, and Spiritual Songs: What the Bible Says about Music*, 2nd ed. Chicago: Cornerstone, 1994.

Verret, Mary Camilla. "A Preliminary Survey of Roman Catholic Hymnals Published in the United States of America." Master's thesis, Catholic University of America, 1964.

Vicky, Schaeffer. "An Historical Survey of Shaker Hymnody Expressing the Christian Virtues of Innocence and Simplicity." DM diss., Indiana University, 1992.

Voigt, Louis, and Ellen Jane Lorenz Porter. *Hymnbook Collections of North America*. Springfield, OH: Hymn Society of America, 1980.

Wright, James Lincoln. "A Study of the Impact of the Chorus on Eight American Protestant Hymnals." Ph.D. diss., Southwestern Baptist Theological Seminary, 1996.

York, Terry Wayne. "Charles Hutchinson Gabriel (1856-1932): Composer, Author, and Editor in the Gospel Tradition." DMA diss., New Orleans Baptist Theological Seminary, 1985.

Young, A. "Apostolate of Congregational Song." *Catholic World* 54 (February 1892): 738-49.

_____. "Why and How of Congregational Singing." *Catholic World* 52 (January 1891): 520-28.

Wasson, D. DeWitt, comp. *Hymntune Index and Related Hymn Materials*. 3 Vols. Lanham, MD: Scarecrow Press, 1998.

Wilhoit, Melvin Ross. "A Guide to the Principal Authors and Composers of Gospel Song of the Nineteenth Century." DMA diss., Southern Baptist Theological Seminary, 1982.

Chapter 14

Amy Beach (Mrs. H. H. A. Beach)

Block, Adrienne Fried. *Amy Beach, Passionate Victorian: the Life and Work of an American Composer, 1867-1944.* New York: Oxford University Press, 1998.

Brittain, Randy Charles. "Festival Jubilate, op. 17 by Amy Cheney Beach (1867-1944): A Performing Edition." DMA diss., University of North Carolina at Greensboro, 1994.

Eden, Myrna Garvey. "Anna Hyatt Huntington, Sculptor, and Mrs. H. H. A. Beach, Composer: A Comparative Study of Two Women Representatives of the American Cultivated Tradition in the Arts." Ph.D. diss., Syracuse University, 1977.

_____. *Energy and Individuality in the Art of Anna Huntington, Sculptor and Amy Beach, Composer.* Metuchen, NJ: Scarecrow Press, 1987.

Jenkins, Walter S., and John H. Baron. *The Remarkable Mrs. Beach, American Composer: A Biographical Account Based on Her Diaries, Letters, Newspaper Clippings, and Personal Reminiscences.* Warren, MI: Harmonie Park Press, 1994. (Detroit Monographs in Musicology. Studies in Music; vol. 13).

Merrill, E. Lindsey. "Mrs. H. H. A. Beach: Her Life and Music." Ph.D. diss., Eastman School of Music of the University of Rochester, 1963.

Reigles, Barbara Jean. "The Choral Music of Amy Beach." Ph.D. diss., Texas Tech University, 1996.

Chapter 15

Dudley Buck

"American Composers: Dudley Buck." *Musician* 1 (1896): 197.

Apthorp, William F. "Centennial Cantata." *Atlantic Monthly* 38, no. 225 (1876): 122.

_____. "The Club Concerts: The Nun of Nidaros." *Musical Herald* 1, no. 4 (1880): 93.

_____. "The Legend of Don Munio." *Atlantic Monthly* 34, no. 206 (1874): 757.

Buck, Albert H. *The Bucks of Wethersfield, Connecticut and the Families with Which They Are Connected by Marriage.* Roanoke, VA: The Stone Printing and Manufacturing Co., 1909.

Buck, Dudley. *Illustrations in Choir Accompaniment with Hints on Registration: A Handbook for the Use of Organ Students, Organists, and Those Interested in Church Music.* New York: G. Schirmer, 1877.

_____. Papers. Library of Congress. Includes over 350 letters.

Dudley Buck: A Complete Bibliography. New York: G. Schirmer, [1910].

Gallo, William K. "The Life and Church Music of Dudley Buck (1839-1909)." Ph.D. diss., Catholic University, 1968.

Hall, James Ramsey. "The Vocal Music of Dudley Buck." Master's thesis, University of North Carolina at Chapel Hill, 1951.

Mathews, W. S. B. "Dudley Buck's Second Collection of Motettes." *Dwight's Journal of Music* 31 (1871): 153-54.

Orr, N. Lee. "Dudley Buck: Leader of a Forgotten Tradition. *The Tracker* 38, no. 3 (Fall 1994): 10-21.

_____. "Edward Hodges, the American Church, and Sacred Music at Mid-Century." *The Tracker* 41, no. 3 (Fall 1995).

Chapter 16

George Chadwick

Campbell, Douglas. "George W. Chadwick: His Life and Works." Ph.D. diss., University of Rochester, 1957.

Engel, Carl. "George W. Chadwick." *Musical Quarterly* 10 (1924): 438-57.

Faucett, Bill F. *George Whitefield Chadwick: A Bio-Bibliography.* Westport, CT: Greenwood Press, 1998.

Langley, Allan Lincoln. "Chadwick and the New England Conservatory of Music." *Musical Quarterly* 21 (January 1935): 39-52.

Yellin, Victor Fell. *Chadwick, Yankee Composer.* Washington: Smithsonian Institution Press, 1990.

Chapter 17

Arthur Foote

Alviani, Doric. "The Choral Church Music of Arthur William Foote."
SMD diss., Union Theological Seminary, 1962.

Cipolla, Wilma Reid. *A Catalog of the Works of Arthur William Foote,
1853-1937.* Detroit: Information Coordinators, 1980.

Foote, Arthur. *Arthur Foote, 1853-1937. An Autobiography.* 1946.
Reprint, with a new introduction by Wilma Reid Cipolla. NY: Da
Capo Press, 1979.

Foote, Arthur, and Albert Israel Elkus. *Arthur Foote Correspondence*
[1922-1927]. 22 letters. Berkeley, CA: University of California.
Correspondence with Albert Elkus, probably 1922-27.

Foote, Arthur. "A Bostonian Remembers." *Musical Quarterly* 33
(January 1937): 37-44.

Foote, Arthur. *The Life and Times of Henry Wilder Foote: 1838-1899.*
Chicago: N.p., 1936.

Hascall, Wilbur. "Arthur Foote." *American Organist* 1 (1918): 300-
301.

Kopp, Frederick Edward. "Arthur Foote, American Composer and
Theorist." Ph.D. diss., Eastman School of Music of the University
of Rochester, 1957.

Tawa, Nicholas E. *Arthur Foote: A Musician in the Frame of Time
and Place.* Lanham, MD: Scarecrow Press, 1997.

Chapter 18

William Wallace Gilchrist

Schleifer, Martha Furman. "William Wallace Gilchrist: Life and Works." Ph.D. diss., Bryn Mawr College, 1976.

_____. *William Wallace Gilchrist, 1846-1916: A Moving Force in the Musical Life of Philadelphia.* Metuchen, NJ: Scarecrow Press, 1985.

_____. "William Wallace Gilchrist: Philadelphia Musician." *Diapason* 72, no. 5 (May 1981): 1, 3, 15.

Chapter 19

Thomas Hastings

Bristol, Lee H., Jr. "Thomas Hastings, 1784-1872." *Hymn* 10, no. 4 (1959): 105-10.

Dooley, James E. "Thomas Hastings: American Church Musician." Ph.D. diss., Florida State University, 1963.

Scanlon, Mary B. "Thomas Hastings." *Musical Quarterly* 32, no. 2 (April 1946): 265-77.

Teal, Mary D. "Letters of Thomas Hastings." *Notes* 24, no. 2 (December 1977): 303-18.

Chapter 20

Anthony Philip Heinrich

Clark, J. Bunker. "Anthony Philip Heinrich: A Bohemian Predecessor to Dvorak in the Wilds of America." In *Dvorak in America: 1892-1894*. Portland, OR: Amadeus, 1993.

Filbeck, Loren Harold. "The Choral Works of Anthony Philip Heinrich." 2 vols. DMA diss., University of Illinois, 1975.

Upton, William Treat. *Anthony Philip Heinrich, a Nineteenth-Century Composer in America*. 1939. Reprint, New York: AMS Press, 1967.

Chapter 21

Lowell Mason

(See also chapter 8)

Doxey, Mary Bitzer. "Lowell Mason, Modern Music Educator." Master's thesis, University of Mississippi, 1957.

Gray, Arlene Elizabeth. "Lowell Mason's Contributions to American Church Music." Master's thesis, University of Rochester, 1941.

Hall, Bonlyn Goodwin. "The American Education of Luther Whiting Mason." *American Music* 6, no. 1 (Spring 1988): 65-73.

Hall, Jack Shelburn. "The Influence of Pestalozzian Theories upon the Music Curriculum of the Early American Common Schools (1830-1860) as Implemented by Horace Mann and Lowell Mason." Ph.D. diss., Indiana University of Pennsylvania, 1981.

Heller, George N. "Lowell Mason (1792-1872) and Music for Students with Disabilities." *Bulletin of Historical Research in Music Education* 16, no. 1 (September 1994): 1-16.

Howell, Lillian Pope. "Lowell Mason, Composer of Hymn-Tunes." Master's thesis, Southern Baptist Theological Seminary, 1948.

Mason, Henry Lowell. *Catalogue of the Lowell Mason Works in Yale School of Music Library*. [New Haven, CT], [1936].

_____. *Hymn-Tunes of Henry Lowell Mason: A Bibliography Compiled by Henry L. Mason*. 1944. Reprint, New York: AMS Press, 1976.

_____. *Musical Letters from Abroad*. Boston: Oliver Ditson and Co., 1858.

_____. *A Yankee Musician in Europe: The 1837 Journals of Lowell Mason*. Edited with an introduction by Michael Broyles. Ann Arbor, MI: University Microfilms International Research Press, 1990.

Mathews, William S. B. "Lowell Mason and the Higher Art of Music in America." *Music: A Monthly Magazine* 9 (1896): 378-88, 575-91.

Moore, Douglas. "The Activities of Lowell Mason in Savannah, Georgia, 1813-1827." Master's thesis, University of Georgia, 1967.

Muradian, Thaddeus George. "Lowell Mason: His Philosophy and Contribution to Music Education." Master's thesis, San Diego State College, 1967.

Nesnow, Adrienne. *Lowell Mason Papers: Yale University Music Library, Archival Collection MSS 33*. New Haven, CT: The Library, 1982.

O'Meara, Eva J. "The Lowell Mason Library." *Notes* 22 (1971): 197-208.

_____. "The Lowell Mason Papers." *Yale University Library Gazette* 45 (1971): 123-26.

Ogasapian, John. "Lowell Mason as a Church Musician." *Journal of Church Music* 21, no. 7 (September 1979): 6-10.

Pemberton, Carol Ann. *Lowell Mason: A Bio-Bibliography*. New York: Greenwood Press, 1988.

_____. *Lowell Mason: His Life and Work*. Ann Arbor, MI: University Microfilms International Research Press, 1985.

Porter, Ellen Jane Lorenz. "A Hymn-Tune Detective Stalks Lowell Mason." *Journal of Church Music* 24, no. 9 (November 1982): 7-11, 31-32.

Rich, Arthur L. "Lowell Mason, Modern Music Teacher." *Music Educators Journal* 23 (January 1942): 22-24.

_____. *Lowell Mason: "The Father of Singing among the Children."* Chapel Hill, NC: University of North Carolina Press, 1946.

Samuel, Harold E. "Rare Resources in the Yale Music Library." *The Library Quarterly* 64, no. 1 (January 1994): 61-72.

Chapter 22

John Knowles Paine

DeVenney, David P. "A Conductor's Study of the Mass in D by John Knowles Paine." DMA diss., University of Cincinnati, 1989.

Harvey, Peter Jon. "German Influences in the Education and Teaching Career of John Knowles Paine." DMA diss., University of Hartford, 1979.

Howe, M. A. DeWolfe. "John Knowles Paine." *Musical Quarterly* 25, no. 3 (July 1939): 257-67.

Huxford, John Calvin. "John Knowles Paine: His Life and Works." Ph.D. diss., Florida State University, 1968.

Roberts, Kenneth C., Jr. "John Knowles Paine." Master's thesis, University of Michigan, 1962.

Schmidt, John C. "The Life and Works of John Knowles Paine." Ph.D. diss., New York University, 1979.

Van Hooser, R. Irving. "John Knowles Paine's *St. Peter*: A Stylistic and Dramatic Analysis." DMA diss., University of Cincinnati, 1994.

Chapter 23

Horatio Parker

Chadwick, George W. *Commemorative Tribute to Horatio Parker, by George Whitefield Chadwick: Read in the 1920 Lecture Series of the American Academy of Arts and Letters*. [New York]: American Academy of Arts and Letters, 1922.

_____. *Horatio Parker, 1863-1920*. 1921. Reprint, New York: AMS Press, 1972.

Kearns, William K. "Horatio Parker, 1863-1919. A Study of His Life and Music." Ph.D. diss., University of Illinois at Urbana-Champaign, 1965.

_____. *Horatio Parker, 1863-1919: His Life, Music, and Ideas*. Metuchen, NJ: Scarecrow Press, 1990.

_____. "Horatio Parker and the English Choral Societies, 1899-1902." *American Music* 4, no. 1 (Spring 1986): 20-33.

_____. "Horatio Parker's Oratorios: A Measure of the Changing Genre at the Turn of the Twentieth Century." *Inter-American Music Review* 11, no. 2 (Spring-Summer 1991): 65-74.

Rorick, William C. "The Horatio Parker Archives in the Yale University Music Library." *Fontes Artis Musicae* 26, no. 4 (1979): 298-304.

Scroggins, Sterling Edward. "The Songs of Horatio Parker: Analysis, History, Anthology, and Recording." DMA diss., University of Maryland at College Park, 1995. Includes discussion of *Hora Novissima*.

Semler, Isabel Parker. *Horatio Parker: A Memoir for His Grandchildren Compiled from Letters and Papers.* New York: Putnam, 1942. Reprint, New York: AMS Press, 1975. Also New York: Da Capo Press, 1973.

Smith, David S. "A Study of Horatio Parker." *Musical Quarterly* 16 (1930): 153- 69.

Chapter 24

Boy Choirs and Male Choral Groups

Albrecht, Theodore. "More than Polkas and Prosit: German Music in Texas." *Texas Humanist* 7, no. 6 (July-August 1985): 26-27, 41.

Arbeiter Männerchor (NY). *See chapter10.*

Cimino, Frank, and Darrell James. "Boychoir." *The Choral Journal* 37, no. 10 (May 1997): 39-40.

Challier, Ernst. *Grösser Männergesang-Katalog.* Giessen: E. Challiers, 1900-1909.

Criswell, Paul Douglas. "The Episcopal Choir School and Choir of Men and Boys in the United States: Its Anglican Tradition, Its American Past and Present." Ph.D. diss., University of Maryland at College Park, 1987.

Duggan, Mary Virginia. "The Boy Choir: A Brief Sketch of Its History in the Church, Together with a Practical Program for its Restoration in a Modern Parish." Master's thesis, University of Notre Dame, 1954.

Dumas, Doyle. "The Männerchor Repertory of the Saxon Colony of Altenburg, Missouri." *Church Music* 2 (1976): 23-36.

Farrell, Michael F. "An Examination of the Training Techniques and Related Factors in Selected Outstanding Boy Choirs in the United States." DMA diss., University of Missouri, Kansas City, 1976.

Goleeke, Wallace John. "I. A History of the Male Chorus Singing Movement in Seattle. II. Problems Encountered in the Preparation for Performance of John Verrall's 'They Shall Never Thirst,' III. 'From the Rubaiyat:' A Cantata for Mixed Chorus, Cello, and Baritone Solo (Original Composition)." DMA diss., University of Washington, 1969.

Hall, Walter Henry. *The Essentials of Boy Choir Training*. New York: Novello, Ewer & Co., [1906].

Howard, Francis E. *The Child-Voice in Singing, Treated From a Physiological and a Practical Standpoint and Especially Adapted to School and Boy Choirs*. New and Rev. ed. New York: H. W. Gray; London: Novello, Ewer & Co., 1898.

Ingerson, Charles F. "The Case of the Boy Choir." SMM, Union Theological Seminary, 1948.

McElvaney, Maude Palmer. "The Place of the Boy Choir in Public Schools." Master's thesis, East Texas State Teachers College, 1940.

Martin, C. G. *Art of Training Choir-Boys*. New York: Novello's Music Primers, 1892.

Moritz, James Paul. "Characteristics and Trends in American and Canadian Boychoirs." Master's thesis, Boston University, 1970.

Powell, James R. *A History of the St. Luke's Boy Choir, 1885-1985*. Kalamazoo, MI: St. Luke's Choristers Centennial Project Committee, St. Luke's Episcopal Church, 1984.

Robins, Robert Patterson. *A Short Sketch of the Orpheus Club of Philadelphia: With a List of the Officers and Members and of the Music Presented at the Concerts*. Philadelphia: [Times Printing House], 1894.

Seidensticker, Oswald. *Geschichte des Männerchors in Philadelphia, 1835-1885*. Philadelphia: Verlag des Männerchors, 1885.

Shepard, Frank Hartson. *Church Music and Choir Training: Treating of the Management of Boys' Voices and the Proper Rendition of Church Music*. Bethel, CT: Frank Hartson Shepard, 1890.

Shirley, Wayne. "American-born Composers of Männerchöre." Unpublished paper read July 9, Oxford, England, as part of "Music in the Nineteenth Century": A joint meeting of the Sonneck Society and the British Biennial Conference on Nineteenth-Century Music, Lady Margaret Hall, Oxford, 8-11 July, 1988.

Snyder, Suzanne G. "The 'Männerchor' Tradition in the United States: A Historical Analysis of Its Contribution to American Musical Culture." Ph.D. diss., University of Iowa, 1991.

Stebbins, Robert A. *The Barbershop Singer: Inside the Social World of a Musical Hobby.* Toronto: University of Toronto Press, 1996.

_____. "Becoming a Barbershop Singer." In *Barbershopping: Musical and Social Harmony.* Rutherford, NJ: Fairleigh Dickinson University Press. London: Associated University Presses, 1993.

Thomas, Arnold Ray. "The Development of Male Glee Clubs in American Colleges and Universities." Ed.D. diss., Columbia University, 1962.

Thorson, Eric Allan. "Collegiate Male Chorus: Curricular Repertoire." Ed.D. diss., Arizona State University, 1982.

Trame, Richard H. "The Male Chorus, Medium of Art and Entertainment: Its History and Literature." In *Choral Essays: A Tribute to Roger Wagner*, ed. William Wells Belan. San Carlos, CA: Thomas House, 1993.

Whitney, S. B. "Surpliced Boy Choirs in America." *New England Magazine* 6 (1892): 139-64.

Chapter 25

Church Histories

Alexander, S. D. *The Presbytery of New York, 1738-1888.* New York: Anson D. F. Randolph and Company, n.d.

Anstice, Henry. *History of St. George's Church in the City of New York, 1752-1911.* New York: Harper & Bros., 1911.

Baker, Robert A., and Paul J. Craven. *Adventure in Faith: The First 300 Years of First Baptist Church, Charleston, South Carolina.* Nashville, Broadman Press, 1982.

Barratt, Norris Stanley. *Outline of the History of Old St. Paul's Church, Philadelphia, Pennsylvania.* [Philadelphia]: The Colonial Society of Pennsylvania, 1917.

Baver, Marlene Jeannette. "The Music of the Cathedral Church of St. Mark, Minneapolis, Minnesota." Master's thesis, Union Theological Seminary, 1955.

Belle, Thomas. *The First Hundred Years, A History of the First Presbyterian Church, Muncie, Indiana.* Muncie, IN: Scott Printing Co., 1938.

Berry, Joseph Breed. *History of the Diocese of Massachusetts, 1810-1872.* Boston: The Diocese Library, The Stinehour Press, 1954.

Blanton, Wyndham B. *The Making of a Downtown Church. The History of the Second Presbyterian Church. Richmond, Virginia. 1845-1945.* Richmond: John Knox Press, 1945.

Bolton, Robert. *History of the Protestant Episcopal Church in the County of Westchester, from Its Foundation, A.D. 1693 to A.D. 1853.* New York: Stanford E. Swords, Publishers, 1855.

Booth, John Nicholls. *The Story of the Second Church of Boston (The Original Old North), Including the Old North Mystery.* Boston: John N. Booth, [1959].

Brown, Roscoe C. E. *Church of the Holy Trinity, Brooklyn Heights, in the City of New York, 1847-1922: An Historical Sketch.* New York: The Dunlap Press, 1922.

Burr, Nelson R. *The Story of the Diocese of Connecticut.* Hartford: Church Missions Publishing Company, 1962.

Carter, Betty Werlein, and Hodding Carter. *So Great a Good: A History of the Episcopal Church in Louisiana and of Christ Church Cathedral, 1805-1955.* Sewanee, TN: The University Press, 1955.

Carthy, Mary Peter. *Old St. Patrick's: New York's First Cathedral.* Thomas J. McMahon, ed. New York: United States Catholic Historical Society, 1947.

Chaney, George Leonard. *Hollis Street Church from Mather Byles to Thomas Starr King, 1732-1861.* Boston: George H. Ellis, 1877.

Chorley, E. Clowes. *The Centennial History of St. Bartholomew's Church in the City of New York.* New York: St. Bartholomew's, 1935.

Church of the Advent (Boston, Mass.). *The Parish of the Advent in the City of Boston, A History of One Hundred Years, 1844-1944.* Boston: Parish of the Advent, 1944.

Clark, Linda Jane. "Music in Trinity Church, Boston, 1890-1990: A Case-Study in the Relationship between Worship and Culture." SMD. diss., Union Theological Seminary, 1973.

Clarkson, David. *History of the Church of Zion and St. Timothy of New York, 1797-1894.* New York: G. P. Putnam's Sons, [1894].

Cook, Leland A. *St. Patrick's Cathedral.* New York: Quick Fox, 1979.

Davis-Rodgers, Ellen. *The Great Book: Calvary Protestant Episcopal Church, Memphis, Tennessee, 1832-1972.* Memphis: The Plantation Press, 1973.

_____. *The Romance of the Episcopal Church in West Tennessee. 1832-1964.* Memphis: The Plantation Press, 1964.

Demille, George E. *A History of the Diocese of Albany.* Philadelphia: Church Historical Society, 1946.

_____. *Saint Thomas Church in the City and County of New York, 1823-1954.* Austin, TX: Church Historical Society, [1958].

The Diocese of Maine 1820-1920. Boston: Merrymount Press, 1920.

Dix, John A. *A History of the Parish of Trinity Church.* New York: G. Putnam, 1950.

Dix, Morgan, John A. Dix, Leicester C. Lewis, Charles T. Bridgeman, Clifford P. Morehouse, eds. *A History of the Parish of Trinity Church in the City of New York.* 7 vols. New York: I: G. P. Putnam's Sons, 1898; II: Knickerbocker Press, 1901; III: G. P. Putnam's Sons, 1905; IV: G. P. Putnam's Sons, 1906; V: Columbia University Press, 1950; VI: Rector, Churchwardens, and Vestrymen, Trinity Church, 1962; VII: Seabury Press, 1978.

Dorr, Benjamin. *A Historical Account of Christ Church, Philadelphia, from Its Foundation, A.D. 1695, to A.D. 1841; and of St. Peter's and St. James's, until the Separation of the Churches.* New York: Swords, Sanford, and Co., 1941.

Duffy, Mark J., ed. *The Episcopal Diocese of Massachusetts, 1784-1984: A Mission to Remember, Proclaim, and Fulfill.* Boston: The Episcopal Diocese of Massachusetts, 1984.

Edmonds, Franklin Spencer. *History of St. Matthew's Church, Francisville, Philadelphia, 1822-1925.* Philadelphia: St. Matthew's Church, Francisville, 1925.

Fisher, George D. *History and Reminiscences of the Monumental Church, Richmond, VA., from 1814-1878.* Richmond: Whittet & Shepperson, 1880.

Fifth Avenue Presbyterian Church (New York, N.Y.). New York: [the church], n.d.

Foote, Henry Wilder, Henry Herbert Edes, John Carroll Perkins, and Warren Winslow. *Annals of Kings Chapel from the Puritan Age of New England to the Present Day.* 3 vols. Boston: Little, Brown, 1882-1940.

Goodrich, Wallace, ed. *The Parish of the Advent in the City of Boston: A History of One Hundred Years, 1844-1944.* Boston: Parish of the Advent, 1944.

Greenleaf, Jonathan. *A History of the Churches of All Denominations in the City of New York: From the First Settlement to the Year 1850.* [Boston]: Beacon Press, [1891].

Griswold, Stephen M. *Sixty Years with Plymouth Church.* New York: Fleming H. Revell Co., 1907.

Hayes, Charles Wells. *The Diocese of Western New York. A History and Recollection.* 2nd ed. Rochester: Scranton, Westmore & Co., 1904.

Higginson, J. Vincent. "Music and Musicians at St. Mary's Church, Philadelphia." *Sacred Music* 109, no. 2 (1982): 13-18.

Hill, Hamilton. *The Early History of the Old South Church (Third Church) Boston, 1669-1884.* New York: Houghton Mifflin, 1890.

Hood, Sebron Yates. "A History of Music at Trinity Church, New York." Master's thesis, Union Theological Seminary, 1955.

Hoogenboom, Olive. *The First Unitarian Church of Brooklyn, One Hundred Fifty Years: A History.* Brooklyn: The Church, 1987.

Inventory of the Church Archives of New Jersey Presbyterians. Historical Records Survey. Newark: Work Projects Administration, 1940.

Knapp, Shepherd. *A History of the Brick Presbyterian Church in the City of New York.* New York: The Trustees of the Brick Presbyterian Church, 1909.

Lindsley, James Elliott. *A History of Saint James Church in the City of New York, 1810-1960.* New York: St. James Church, 1960.

Lord, Robert Howard. *History of the Archdiocese of Boston in the Various Stages of Its Development, 1604-1943.* Boston: Pilot Pub. Co., 1945.

MacAdam, George. *The Little Church around the Corner.* New York: G. P. Putnam's Sons, 1925.

Malone, Henry T. *The Episcopal Church in Georgia, 1733-1957.* Atlanta: The Protestant Episcopal Church in the Diocese of Atlanta, [1960].

Messiter, Arthur Henry. *A History of the Choir and Music of Trinity Church, New York, from Its Organization, to the Year 1897.* 1906. Reprint, New York: AMS Press, [1970].

Moleck, Fred J. "Nineteenth Century Musical Activity at St. Vincent Archabbey, Latrobe, Pennsylvania." Ph.D. diss., University of Pittsburgh, 1970.

Morris, J. Wesley. *Christ Church, Cincinnati, 1817-1967.* Cincinnati: The Episcopal Society of Christ Church, 1967.

Ogasapian, John. [Trinity Church, NY] *See chapter 9.*

Otis, Philo Adam. *The First Presbyterian Church, 1833-1913; A History of the Oldest Organization in Chicago.* 2nd rev. ed., Chicago: Fleming H. Revell Co., 1913.

Owen, Barbara. *The Organs and Music of King's Chapel, 1713-1991.* 2nd ed. Boston: King's Chapel, 1993.

Parish History and Year Book of the Church of the Epiphany: Ashland Boulevard and Adams Street, Chicago. Chicago: Payne & Payne, 1897.

Parker, Edwin Pond. *History of the Second Church of Christ in Hartford.* Hartford, CT: Belknap & Warfield, 1892.

Peek, Richard Maurice. "A Brief History of Music at the Church of the Ascension, New York City." Master's thesis, Union Theological Seminary, 1952.

Peters, John Punnett, ed. *Annals of St. Michael's.* New York: G. P. Putnam's Sons, 1907.

Perkins, J. Newton. *History of the Parish Church of the Incarnation, New York, City 1852-1912.* Poughkeepsie, NY: Frank B. Howard Press, 1912.

Pierce, Roderic Hall. *Trinity Cathedral Parish. The First 150 Years.* Cleveland: Vestry of Trinity Cathedral, 1967.

Reynolds, Helen Wilkinson, ed. *The Records of Christ Church, Poughkeepsie, New York.* 2 vols. Poughkeepsie, NY: Frank B. Howard, [1911-?].

Ritter, Abraham. *History of the Moravian Church in Philadelphia: From Its Foundation in 1742 to the Present Time.* Philadelphia: Hayes & Zell, 1857.

Romig, Edgar Dutcher. *The Story of Trinity Church, in the City of Boston.* Boston: Wardens & Vestry, 1964.

Rothsteiner, John Ernest. *History of the Archdiocese of St. Louis: In Its Various Stages of Development from A.D. 1673 to A.D. 1928.* St. Louis: Blackwell Wielandy, 1928.

Shepherd, Massey Hamilton, Jr. *History of St. James Church, Chicago A.D. 1834-1934.* Chicago: privately printed [The Lakeside Press], 1934.

Shoemaker, Samuel. *Calvary Church Yesterday and Today.* New York: Felmen H. Revell Company, 1936.

Shultz, Rima Lunin. *The Church and the City: A Social History of 150 Years at Saint James, Chicago.* Chicago: the Cathedral of St. James, 1986.

A Sketch of the History of the Parish of the Advent in the City of Boston, 1844-1894. Boston: Parish of the Advent, 1894.

Smith, David Neal. "History of Music, the Church of the Holy Trinity, Brooklyn, New York." Master's thesis, Union Theological Seminary, 1955.

Smith, Franklin Campbell. *The Diocese of Western Michigan. A History.* Grand Rapids: Diocesan Historical Commission, 1948.

Smythe, George Franklin. *A History of the Diocese of Ohio until the Year 1918.* Cleveland: published by the Diocese, 1931.

Stewart, William Rhinelander. *Grace Church and Old New York.* New York: E. P. Dutton & Co., [1924].

Stockwell, George Appleton, and Louis D. Norton. *Our Choir. By the Sexton . . . Assisted by Geo. A. Stockwell.* Providence: William J. Danielson, [1890].

Teichert, Adolph. "Some Notes on the Music at St. Mary-the-Virgin, New York City, 1870-1906." Master's thesis, Union Theological Seminary, 1953.

Thomas, Albert S. *A Historical Account of the Protestant Episcopal Church in South Carolina, 1820-1957.* Columbia, SC: R. L. Bryan Co., 1957.

Thompson, Noyes L. *The History of Plymouth Church: (Henry Ward Beecher) 1847-1872.* New York: G. W. Carleton & Co., 1873.

Trautmann, Jean Elizabeth. "A History of Music at Saint Bartholomew's Church, New York." Master's thesis, Union Theological Seminary, 1951.

Trinity Church, Princeton, New Jersey: A History in Celebration of 150 Years, 1833-1983. Princeton, NJ: Barracks Press, 1988.

Tuttle, Penelope, and T. Sturgis Cook. *History of Saint Luke's Church in the City of New York, 1820-1920.* New York: Appeal Printing Co., 1926.

Twelves, J. Wesley. *A History of the Diocese of Pennsylvania of the Protestant Episcopal Church in the U.S.A., 1784-1968.* Philadelphia: The Diocese of Pennsylvania, 1969.

Wagner, Harold Ezra. *The Episcopal Church in Wisconsin, 1847-1947: A History of the Diocese of Milwaukee.* Waterloo, WI: Courier Printing Co., 1947.

Walker, George Leon. *History of the First Church in Hartford, 1633-1883.* Hartford: Brown & Gross, 1884.

Ward, Susan Hayes. *The History of the Broadway Tabernacle Church: From its Organization in 1840 to the Close of 1900, Including Factors Influencing Its Formation.* New York: [The Trow Printing Company], 1901.

Warlick, Roger K. *As Grain Once Scattered: The History of Christ Church, Savannah, Georgia, 1733-1983.* Columbia: The State Printing Company, 1987.

Washburn, Louis C. *Christ Church, Philadelphia.* Philadelphia: Macrae, Smith, Co., 1925.

Weddell, Elizabeth Wright. *St. Paul's Church, Richmond Virginia, Its Historic Years and Memorials.* 2 vols. Richmond, VA: The William Byrd Press, 1931.

Wilson, James Grant, ed. *The Centennial History of the Protestant Episcopal Church in the Diocese of New York, 1785-1885.* New York: D. Appleton and Co., 1886.

Wolfgang, Ralph T. *The Episcopal Church in Central Pennsylvania.* Harrisburg: Diocese of Central Pennsylvania, 1971.

Wood, Nathan E. *The History of the First Baptist Church of Boston (1665-1899).* Philadelphia: American Baptist Publication Society, 1899.

Weisiger, Minor T., Donald R. Traser, and E. Randolph Trice. *Not Hearers Only: A History of St. James's Episcopal Church, Richmond, Virginia, 1835-1985.* Richmond: St. James's Episcopal Church, 1986.

Wright, Helen Martha. *Two Hundredth Anniversary, Reminiscences of the First Presbyterian Church, Mendham, New Jersey, 1738-1938.* Jersey City: H. M. Wright, 1938.

Year Book of St. George's Church, 1880-1881. New York: New York Public Library, 1990.

Chapter 26

Philosophy, Sermons, and Talks

Bailey, Shelory Cecil. *A Sermon on Music*. Midlothian, TX: Argus Printing Houses, 1899.

Baltimore Pastor. *Church Music: An Address to Presbyterians*. Baltimore: S. Guiteau, Tract Depository, 1857. Microfilm.

Bartlett, Joseph. *Music as an Auxiliary to Religion: An Address before the Handel Society of Dartmouth College, April 1841*. Boston: Crocker and Brewster, 1841.

Bispham, Calrence Wyatt. *Practical Suggestions on Church Music for the Younger Clergy*. . . . N.p., [1897?].

Blagden, George Washington. *An Address before the Associate Choirs of the Evangelical Churches, Boston, Bowdoin St. Church, Oct. 24, 1840*. Boston: Perkins & Marvin, 1840.

Blodgett, Benjamin Colman. *The Place of Music in Public Worship. An Address Delivered before the Worcester Congregational Club, Worcester, Mass., November 16th, 1885, by Benjamin C. Bledgett.* Boston: T. Todd Printer, 1886.

Chadwick, John White. *The Choir Invisible: A Sermon*. Boston: George H. Ellis, 1897.

Crafts, Wilbur F. *Trophies of Song: Articles and Incidents on the Power of Sacred Music* . . . Boston: D. Lothrop & Co., [1874].

Dana, Daniel. *An Address on Sacred Musick, Delivered at a Publick Meeting of the Rockingham Sacred Musick Society*. . . . Exeter, NH: Charles Norris & Co., 1813.

Greenlea, P. *The Office of Music in the Church of God.* . . . Cincinnati: Moore, Wilstach, 1856.

Hall, Charles Henry. *Of the Use of Art in the Music of the Church: Two Discourses Preached in the Church of the Holy Trinity, Brooklyn, New York*. Brooklyn: N.p., 1876.

Hastings, Thomas. *Dissertation on Musical Taste; or, General Principles of Taste Applied to the Art of Music*. New Introduction by James E. Dooley. 1822. Reprint, New York: Da Capo, 1974.

Hewins, James M. *Hints Concerning Church Music, the Liturgy and Kindred Spirits*. Boston: Ide & Dutton, 1856.

Hodge, Charles Russell. *Clergy and Choir*. Milwaukee: Young Churchman Co., 1891.

Hodges, Edward. *An Essay on the Cultivation of Church Music*. New York: A. J. Sparks, 1841.

Hooker, Edward W. *A Plea for Sacred Music: A Premium Tract*. New York: American Tract Society, [1850?]

_____. *An Address, Delivered before the Hastings and Mason Musical Association, at Pittsfield, December 25, 1837*. Pittsfield: P. Allen and Son, 1838.

_____. *An Address Delivered before the Society of Sacred Music, in the Theol. Seminary of East Windsor, August 6, 1839*. New York: J. F. Trow, 1839.

_____. *An Address on Sacred Music: Delivered at Castleton, Sept. 28th, 1843*. Montpelier, VT: E. P. Walton & Sons, 1843.

Hubbard, John. *An Essay on Music: Pronounced before the Middlesex Musical Society, Sept. 9, A.D. 1807, at Dunstable, (Mass.)*. Boston: Manning & Loring, 1808.

Jones, Robert Ellis. *"Music in the Church Service:" Essay Read before the Michigan Music Teacher's Association at Detroit, June 28, 1889, by Rev. Robert Ellis Jones*. . . . [Detroit? 1889?].

Lyon, William Henry. *Church Music*. Boston: N.p., [1894?].

Lucas, G. W. *Remarks on the Musical Conventions in Boston, &c.* Northampton, MA: printed for the author, 1844.

Mason, Lowell. *Address on Church Music.* . . . Boston: Hilliard, Gray, and Company, 1826.

_____. *Song in Worship*. Orange, NJ: printed for private circulation, 1888.

Mulchahey, James. *A Plea for Truth in Church Music*. New York: N. p., [1881].

Nevin, John Williamson. *Address on Sacred Music: Delivered at the Anniversary of the Handel and Hastings Society in the Theological Seminary, Princeton, N. J., Dec. 5, 1827.* Princeton, NJ: D. A Borrenstein, 1827.

Oberley, Henry Harrison. *Church Music. An Address in St. Agnes Chapel, New York, before the Faculty and Students of the General Theological Seminary.* New York: Trow Printing Co., 1893.

Phelps, Austin. *Hymns and Choirs; or the Matter and the Manner of the Service of Song in the House of the Lord.* . . . Andover, MA: W.   F. Draper, 1860.

Porter, Eliphalet Nott. "Music and Worship." *Princeton Review* (July 1879): 127-43.

Resolution of the House of Bishops, on the Subject of Music in the Church. New York: J. F. Trow, 1859.

Schieffelin, Samuel Brandhurst. *A Letter to the Elders in the Reformed Church, by Samuel B. Schieffelin.* New York: Reform Church of America, 1881.

Steele, James Nevett. *The Importance of Musical Knowledge to the Priesthood of the Church.* New York: J. Pott and Co., 1894.

Swope, C.E. *The Music of the Church: An Address Delivered . . . in Trinity Chapel . . . Nov. 18, 1880.* New York: H. J. Hewitt, 1880.

Whittingham, Richard. *Choir Unions, or Musical Festivals; Being Some Suggestions for the Improvement of Church Music.* New York: H. B. Durand, 1863.

Wienandt, Elwyn Arthur, comp. *Opinions on Church Music; Comments and Reports from Four-and-a-Half Centuries.* Waco, TX: Markham Press Fund of Baylor University, 1974.

Index

About The Authors

N. Lee Orr, Ph.D., is professor of music and chair of music history and literature at Georgia State University in Atlanta. He writes on American music, most recently with his *Alfredo Barili and the Rise of Classical Music in Atlanta*, (Scholars Press, 1996). He is currently working on an edition of Victorian American choral music by Dudley Buck as well as a study of the rise of choral music in nineteenth-century America.

W. Dan Hardin, DMA, is periodicals/music liaison librarian at Georgia State University. In addition to a master's degree in library and information service, he holds the doctor of musical arts degree in organ performance and literature from the Eastman School of Music, and the master of music degree from Northwestern University. Dr. Hardin writes on online research methodology and remains active as a recitalist and accompanist.